Royal Horticultural Society

Sharing the best in Gardening

THE URBAN GARDENER

Royal Horticultural Society
Sharing the best in Gardening

THE URBAN GARDENER

MATT JAMES

Photography by Marianne Majerus

MITCHELL BEAZLEY

For my budding gardeners, Frankie and Rosie.

RHS The Urban Gardener
Matt James

First published in Great Britain in 2014 by Mitchell Beazley,
an imprint of Octopus Publishing Group Ltd, Endeavour House,
189 Shaftesbury Avenue, London WC2H 8JY
www.octopusbooks.co.uk

An Hachette UK Company
www.hachette.co.uk

Published in association with the Royal Horticultural Society, London

Distributed in the US by Hachette Book Group USA,
237 Park Avenue, New York NY 10017 USA

Distributed in Canada by Canadian Manda Group,
165 Dufferin Street, Toronto, Ontario, Canada M6K 3H6

ISBN: 978 1 84533 796 4

A CIP record for this book is available from the British Library.

Set in Champion, MuseoSlab, Strada and Veneer.

Printed and bound in China.

Publisher: Alison Starling
Senior Editor: Leanne Bryan
Copy Editor: Joanna Chisholm
Proofreader: Mandy Greenfield
Indexer: Helen Snaith
Art Director: Jonathan Christie
Senior Art Editor: Juliette Norsworthy
Designer: Lizzie Ballantyne
Picture Library Manager: Bennet Smith
Assistant Production Manager: Caroline Alberti

RHS Publisher: Rae Spencer-Jones
RHS Consultant Editor: Simon Maughan

The Royal Horticultural Society is the UK's leading gardening charity
dedicated to advancing horticulture and promoting good gardening.
Its charitable work includes providing expert advice and information,
training the next generation of gardeners, creating hands-on
opportunities for children to grow plants, and conducting research
into plants, pests and environmental issues affecting gardeners.
For more information, visit: www.rhs.org.uk or call 0845 130 4646.

CONTENTS

INTRODUCTION

At first glance, the typical urban garden seems like a by-product of urban planning and design that stretches back decades. Small in size and beset by problems such as lack of privacy, pollution and shade, an urban garden can present many challenges. The good news is that these can all be overcome so that something stunningly beautiful results from your creative efforts. Your plot may be an untapped oasis, ripe for the gardening.

Your urban garden matters. It can extend your living space, be a safe play area for children and transform itself into an alfresco delight for entertaining family and friends. The garden is a place for your soul, as well as your body, to find rest and relaxation. There's no better area to soothe tired minds and bodies after a stressful day.

But greening your garden isn't just about you; the implications spread far wider. A well-tended garden actually enriches the lives of those all around you – not just the neighbours, but the wider community, including wildlife too.

And what about the environment? Sustainability, carbon emissions, food miles, water use and recycling, pesticides and wildlife – to name but a few – have never been more important issues to consider. Both you and your garden can make a real difference. But this doesn't mean that all urban gardens should be allowed to grow 'wild' and untamed. Ecofriendly design can still be clean, crisp and cutting edge. In these pages you'll find numerous contemporary examples in all shapes and guises, from basements to exposed, high-rise roof terraces, and everything in between.

My aim here is to inspire you with simple practical advice on how to make the most of your urban garden, regardless of the size of your budget, how much time-to-tend you have and whether the area is as big as a tennis court or as small as a shoebox. In fact, you might not even possess a garden at all, but instead have a collection of colourful containers outside the front door – even a windowbox has boundless potential.

Whatever you've got, cherish and appreciate its importance. With resolve and a little enthusiasm it's completely possible to transform any space, giving deep satisfaction to the creator and untold pleasure to all who seek a green haven in the urban environment.

A NOTE FROM THE RHS

At the Royal Horticultural Society, we are passionate about gardening. And with more than 90 percent of people living in urban areas in the UK, a key aim is to support town- and city-dwellers to make the most of their plots by providing inspirational advice and information. This is backed by our scientific research programme, which has already shown that urban gardens offer benefits ranging from preventing flooding to providing homes for wildlife. For more information, visit **www.rhs.org.uk/urbangreening**.

Opposite: A gorgeous green garden will enhance city living whether you're inside or out.

GARDENING ON THE LEDGE

This book shows you how to make the most of your urban garden. Before you delve deep into the details of the planning and planting, it's important to appreciate the wider environment. You and your garden are part of a much bigger picture.

Urban greening

Urban greening isn't a new concept – the benefits of plants to towns and cities have been recognised by many urban planners and landscape architects, for decades. However, with climate change and justifiable concerns about energy use and the loss of biodiversity, urban gardens, the plants in them and the important role they have to play have never been more widely appreciated.

You may question the value of your individual impact, but if every resident in every property, on every street, made a conscious effort the results would be staggering. Remember, it all adds up! Your garden does matter. Plants and gardens help in the following ways.

• Addressing the carbon question

In towns and cities, air pollution is impossible to ignore. Factories, planes and road vehicles pump out sulphur dioxide, carbon monoxide, carbon dioxide and nitrogen dioxide, and together with harmful particulates (including brake dust and carbon emitted during the combustion process) cover buildings in layers of dirt. Leaves trap airborne impurities which, following rainfall, are washed into the soil. Plants are the 'lungs' of a city too; trees in particular 'breathe in' huge amounts of carbon dioxide as part of the natural photosynthetic process. Plants with powerful free-scented flowers can also provide relief from obnoxious smells.

How much urban domestic gardens act as a carbon 'sink' or how much carbon gardens and gardening emit is unclear. Some scientists actually suggest that overall more carbon is emitted through the creation and maintenance of a garden than if gardening wasn't done at all. However, this does depend on the style and how the garden is managed. To reduce your carbon footprint is pretty straightforward. Use locally sourced materials, propagate as many plants as you can, plant a tree (trees absorb huge amounts of carbon) and go organic. Don't cut down mature trees unless they are dangerous, and don't water and feed your lawn. Do use a push mower (not an electric or petrol model), turn down greenhouse heaters and make your own compost.

• Urban cooling

Compared to rural locations towns and cities are hot and getting unbearably hotter. Concrete, brick and tarmac absorb solar radiation – contributing to a phenomenon known as the 'heat island effect' –

Opposite: An oasis atop the city streets. Imagine if we all greened our gardens like this...

Right: Lawns, planted beds, trees and surfaces such as permeable paving, bark and gravel absorb heavy rain and allow water to drain naturally into the soil, rather than run off too fast and thereby contribute to localised flooding.

while vegetation reflects it; of course trees provide shade too. A warmer temperature (most noticeably at night) might mean tender plants need less cosseting through the winter, but it also results in earlier flowering, the need for more water and the enhanced possibility of an attack from aggressive pests and diseases that relish the warmer conditions.

• Flood control & rainwater management

Unlike impermeable paving and pavements, soil and grass absorb rainwater, thereby helping to reduce localised flooding. Plants, most notably trees, intercept rain and slow its passage to the ground, which in turn alleviates the pressure on storm drains.

• Reducing energy costs & enhancing thermal insulation

Plants and trees don't just cool the air; they cool buildings in summer and warm them in winter, saving energy used to fuel air conditioning and central heating. Green roofs and living walls (using climbers or specially designed, wall-mounted modules; see p144) are ideal.

Trees, notably deciduous species, are particularly useful: in summer they cool with their shade; and in winter, when the leaves are lost, they allow warming sunlight to reach buildings. Positioned carefully, trees and hedges can gently funnel the wind to cool buildings or act as a windbreak, tempering any adverse effects.

• Conserving water

Water is a precious resource, and with climate change and rising urban temperatures water shortages are only set to increase. Try to conserve or use recycled water wherever possible. For more information on water conservation see p210.

• Urban wildlife & biodiversity

Wildlife is a treasure to cherish, and the urban garden can support all manner of birds, animals and insects. With urbanisation increasing year on year, more and more natural habitats are under threat. A simple change in gardening practice – reducing pesticide use, for example – and the kind of plants you grow can be a massive help in alleviating this loss of habitats.

Above: Piles of dead wood left stacked in the garden provide homes during winter for frogs and newts. They also encourage stag beetles, ground beetles, rove beetles, slowworms and centipedes, all of which feast on slugs and slug eggs.

Left: Living walls not only look attractive but also help keep buildings cool in summer, and warmer in winter, by insulating them and so reducing the need for air conditioning and central heating.

Below: Small dry ponds or 'swales', where the water level ebbs and flows depending on the weather, help to manage storm-water run-off and can present stunning design opportunities too, even on a small scale.

GREENING IS GOOD

22.7 million households (87 percent of homes) in the UK have access to a garden. What you do in your garden can really add up.[1]

Gardens account for about a quarter of the land in the UK's towns and cities. Together they make a significant 'green' contribution to our neighbourhoods.[2]

An increase in plants of just 10 percent would help control the rise in summertime air temperatures predicted with climate change.[3]

Homes with poorly insulated walls (without cavities) particularly benefit from an insulation-like layer of climbers. It's been found that this can help reduce heating bills.[4]

Small, city-centre gardens support similar invertebrate wildlife (such as worms, insects and spiders) to larger suburban ones.[5]

Some declining species such as the common frog, song thrushes and hedgehogs, once abundant in low-intensity farmland, are now more often found in urban areas.[6]

Urban gardens can be home to more than 250 species of wildlife. One 30-year study of a UK garden in Leicestershire found 1,997 insects, 138 invertebrates (such as spiders and woodlice), 54 species of birds and 7 mammals.[7]

Gardening can contribute indirectly to carbon emissions through the consumption of manufactured and transported horticultural goods, and through the use of power tools. Aim to minimise these where possible.[8]

Domestic gardens contain approximately 25 percent of the total of non-forest and woodland trees and can contribute as much as 86 percent of the total urban tree stock.[9]

Every year, hard surfaces in gardens increase by twice the area of London's Hyde Park, which covers 142ha (350 acres).[10]

Data from warmer regions of the world (Mediterranean, Australia) suggest that, as temperatures rise, the proportion of household water used in the garden will increase by more than 30 percent.[11]

Note For details of sources, see p224.

Left: Plants are without doubt the greatest tool available to gardeners and help with the many environmental problems we face in contemporary society.

Assessing your garden

Like a jigsaw, your garden has various factors and features that combine to create different microclimates, while other factors might determine the aesthetic or significantly affect how much you end up spending. Before jumping knee deep into a new design it pays to spend time analysing the space, and considering what you've got. An open mind is essential; some things might seem like problems at first, but they could be opportunities for interesting design. In the previous few pages we've looked at some factors to consider. Now let's assess particularly those that are local to your garden.

Aspect & orientation

The amount of light a garden receives is determined by its aspect; this significantly affects the plants you can grow. A compass will help here. South-facing gardens receive lots of light, while light hits east-facing ones mainly in the morning. West-facing plots get sun in the afternoon and early evening, and north-facing gardens receive the least sunlight. In small gardens it's likely you'll grow most plants on surrounding walls and fences, so note the orientation of each boundary too.

• **North-facing boundaries**
These are generally cold and shady, receiving little direct sunlight.

• **South-facing boundaries**
When combined with free-draining sandy soil, plants here can dry out quickly in the warm or hot conditions.

• **East-facing boundaries**
These are often cold. They catch the early morning sun, which can be difficult for evergreens such as camellias, as the leaves get scorched.

• **West-facing boundaries**
These receive sun in the afternoon and evening; they provide the best position for more tender plants.

Another key factor of aspect and orientation is the effect surrounding trees and buildings have on your space. Trees could shade it most of the day, making a south-facing garden feel more like a north-facing one. Or neighbouring buildings clad with mirrored glass might reflect lots of light into otherwise gloomy corners. It pays to spend a day in a deckchair (any excuse!) and identify which areas are shadier than others when the sun moves around the garden.

Above: A shady area in the garden is a wonderful opportunity to plant gorgeous woodlanders like fringe cups (*Tellima grandiflora*), ferns, columbine (*Aquilegia*), foxgloves (*Digitalis*) and wood cranesbill (*Geranium sylvaticum* 'Mayflower'). Don't see it as being all doom and gloom.

Exposure

Strong winds can make it uncomfortable to sit outside, and they can wreak havoc on plants, breaking stems and leaves and seriously reducing a plant's ability to reproduce. The drying effect also desiccates tender foliage. Therefore it is important to note the prevailing wind direction in your garden.

A word of warning: surrounding buildings, which could funnel or deflect strong winds, have a huge impact. Similarly, a wall around your garden offers shelter but one running across the prevailing wind will create swirling 'eddies' on the leeward side. It's better to use hedges or to erect hit-and-miss fencing here – being permeable, these moderate and diffuse the wind.

Soil

No gardening book is complete without a mention of the importance of soil. It filters and cleans water, absorbs gases such as carbon dioxide and provides a habitat for key members of the food chain. Of course, it supports plants too.

I'm not going to give you a soil science lesson here – the chances are you know much of it already. If not, there's lots of online content or books that go into the details. But I will say this: spend some time getting to know your soil. Learn how it behaves, whether it drains well or gets waterlogged, whether it's thick and difficult to dig (likely with clay soil) or if it's dry and dusty (probably soil with a high proportion of silt or sand). This way you can learn how to manage it effectively for the best results (for more on this, see the Managing the Urban Garden chapter).

Your garden's soil will behave differently under trees, by walls or in the lee of surrounding buildings, so don't just note how it performs in one spot. If you are creating a garden around a newly built property, the chances are that the nutrient-rich topsoil (the uppermost soil layer) has been buried or polluted when the builders dug out the building's foundations; you may also discover that the garden has been compacted by heavy machinery,

meaning you'll need to dig deeply where planting is planned in order to revive it. Add lots of compost as you dig to aerate the soil further and top up fertility levels.

Colour also provides clues to soil behaviour. Soils rich in organic matter will be dark brown/black, delightfully crumbly and easy to work. Soils that drain poorly have a mottled grey, blue-black or reddish appearance the deeper you dig.

Left: For *Ligularia* 'The Rocket', goatsbeard (*Aruncus dioicus*), variegated dogwood (*Cornus alba* 'Elegantissima') and coyote willow (*Salix exigua*) to thrive like this, damp, often clay-rich soil is essential.

Below: Soil isn't just a medium for growing plants; you can make rammed-earth walls from it too – one of the oldest, most sustainable building techniques in the world.

pH

The acidity or alkalinity of soil is measured horticulturally by its pH level. The pH level of soil affects the availability of certain nutrients. Some plants such as camellias and rhododendrons prefer acid soils (with a pH of less than 7). Others such as clematis and lilac (*Syringa*) prefer alkaline (often chalky) conditions (with a pH of more than 7). Use a simple test kit from a garden centre to find out. If your soil means you can't grow favourites, plant them instead in containers filled with the right compost (see p192). It is possible to amend the pH – adding lime to make soil more alkaline, or sulphur to make it more acidic – but the soil will revert back over time, so this isn't a long-term solution.

Existing features

Very few gardens I know of are a complete 'blank canvas' so it's unlikely you'll need to start a design totally from scratch. Spend time noting the position and condition of existing features. Some might need replacing, because they're dangerous, dated or decrepit, while others could be the inspiration for a new design proposal or perhaps be included in new plans. That said, evaluate the condition and appearance of structural features like paths, patios, walls (particularly retaining walls) and fences. Replace these before planting borders and laying brand-new lawns.

The 'borrowed' landscape

Your garden might not have views to rolling fields or a fine cityscape (balconies and roof terraces like the one below being the obvious exception) but see your garden as part of a bigger picture and take into account the landscape immediately around you, particularly the gardens on either side. Colourful climbers atop walls and fences and overhanging trees are visually all part of your space too. Embrace them with complementary shrubs and perennials and blur the boundaries between your garden and the next, in turn making it feel a whole lot bigger.

Mature plants

Maturity is an asset to any garden. Provided they are healthy, always keep mature trees and large shrubs if you can, because replacing them is expensive and their removal might reveal a gap that is hard to fill. Overgrown evergreens close to the house may need to be removed for security reasons, but those further away might be usefully masking an eyesore.

Coping with concrete

A garden covered in concrete might feel like a nightmare, but it can be transformed. But do you cover it, remove it or a bit of both? If access is poor and machinery cannot be used, digging out a thick concrete pad manually is time-consuming, back-breaking work. Instead, consider covering the concrete with decking, the sub-frame suspended just above the concrete base. Concrete in good condition might also be the perfect foundation for terracotta tiles or thin paving – as long as adding these won't compromise the damp-proof course of the building.

  If there is a smooth, crack-free surface, concrete paint is another option for transforming the space. Acid staining, a technique popular in the USA, which leaves

Above: Cutting back the branches of overhanging trees to your boundary line is one option, but this will disfigure the tree and be ugly to look at. Instead, cherish such limbs for their size and stature. Of course, there can be other benefits too!

Left: On balconies and roof terraces views like this should be embraced. Here, the containers and the cedar panelling forge links to the patterns found in the architecture beyond.

a blotchy appearance that doesn't look like concrete, is also possible. However, it should be applied only by experienced professionals.

If you do decide on removing any concrete, you'll then need to address the 'dead' soil underneath. The chances are that much of the fertile topsoil will have been taken away before the hardscaping was laid, leaving only the infertile subsoil. Any remaining topsoil buried under a concrete cap will be sterile, compacted and generally in poor shape. Again the options are to repair or replace.

On a small scale – such as borders for planting cut out around the perimeter of a concrete-covered courtyard – it's possible to dig down to 25–30cm (10–12in) and replace the soil with high-quality topsoil mixed with well-rotted garden compost.

On a larger scale extensive soil replacement would be prohibitively expensive. Instead, deeply cultivate the soil (ideally to the depth of a spade blade), incorporating lots of garden compost as you go, to improve soil structure and background fertility levels. When you plant, consider mixing some mycorrhizal fungi powder into the planting hole too; this may establish a mutually beneficial relationship with plant roots, helping plants to take up water and nutrients more quickly.

Access

Before undertaking any major work it is important to consider the access points to your garden, as they influence not only the size of the materials you choose but also the design itself. If access is possible only through the house, clearance work in the garden should be kept to a minimum. Consider a design that avoids the necessity of digging out tons of soil or concrete by hand (although a microdigger might squeeze through a building if the building has concrete floors).

If you are planning lots of work in the garden, try to avoid damage to thoroughfares by protecting door frames, radiators and internal walls using thick plastic sheeting with thin hardboard on top, fixed together with duct tape.

Right: Where concrete is tricky to remove or shouldn't be removed (on a roof terrace, for example), decking can be built over the top. However, on a balcony or roof terrace just make sure it won't raise the surface too much and contravene the minimum railing where you live.

Above: Running water can help mask city sounds, just make sure it's not too powerful, or you might replace one nuisance noise with another.

Noise pollution

Noise pollution is highly subjective. A mower can merely be a nuisance for some people, but extremely annoying for others. But for those living close to busy roads, railways or airports, noise pollution is a serious problem. Plants really help deaden the din, but planting must be as dense as possible. Not only does screening the source of the sound lessen its impact, but plants and soil also absorb sound while solid surfaces bounce it around. Where space is tight, achieving a significant decibel drop is difficult, because there isn't room for extensive planting. Living walls (see p144) or 'acoustic' walls, covered in climbers and erected in a similar way to traditional fencing, can help here.

Running water and tall plants such as bamboos and grasses, which rustle in the breeze, can provide distraction, but avoid powerful and therefore noisy water features.

Privacy

A lack of privacy dramatically affects how much time you spend in your garden. Total privacy is virtually impossible, and maintaining decent light levels is tricky too; however a little trade-off here is necessary, whatever you do. Usually it's enough to concentrate your efforts on screening specific doors or windows belonging to neighbouring properties that overlook your garden – a carefully placed tree might be all that's needed. Sometimes, the mere suggestion of privacy is enough – a pergola or line of pleached hedges (hedges on stilts) 'ceiling' a space should parry all but the most inquisitive neighbours.

With tall buildings overlooking your space, private rooms within the garden, created using canvas shade-sails, a pergola or louvre-style panels erected overhead (with slats positioned at an oblique angle), are useful. Freestanding trellis is an inexpensive option and also lets in light while keeping out ugly views. Note the size of the holes before you buy the trellis – the smaller they are, the less you can see, with or without climbers.

Plants too are perfect for providing privacy. For an 'instant' screen choose large pleached hedges, bamboos (buy clump-formers such as *Chusquea* and *Fargesia* rather than invasive 'running' bamboos such as *Phyllostachys* and *Pseudosasa*) and tidy evergreen trees, including bull bay (*Magnolia grandiflora*).

Left, top: Overhead beams or a pergola draped in climbers suggest privacy overhead and help to 'ceiling' a space. And they don't cut out too much light.

Left: Tall planting creates privacy and screens ugly eyesores. But planting at this height takes time to grow and isn't an instant option. If immediacy is required buy big plants or design private rooms in the garden, rather than trying to enclose the whole thing.

WHAT DOES THE URBAN GARDEN LOOK LIKE?

Over the years urban gardens have evolved from being places concerned with growing plants and getting close to Mother Nature to ones in which human wants and needs take priority. In extreme cases this has resulted in stripped-back designs dominated by hardscape.

Recently, however, gardeners have identified ways in which the two approaches can coexist, even in the smallest spaces. An equilibrium has been found between the traditional role of the garden and its modern incarnation as an 'outdoor room'.

This subtle shift isn't just down to a passing trend; the philosophy behind garden-making itself has changed, having a big impact on both the design process and the aesthetic. On the one hand, art and other design disciplines now inspire designers to reinvent traditional concepts, while, on the other hand, environmental concerns like water management and energy use have a marked influence too.

What is the sustainable garden?

Sustainability is the buzz word for the new zeitgeist. Put simply, sustainable gardening is the attempt to create and maintain a garden while causing as little damage to the environment as possible. To me, a sustainable garden is: one that exists in harmony with the natural world; a garden that reduces its impact on, and seeks out alternatives to, finite resources (water and peat, for example); and one where unnecessary intervention is kept to a minimum.

The sustainable 'look'

Contrary to popular belief, sustainable gardens don't have to be informal and full of wild flowers. Crisp modern designs also tick many sustainable boxes simply by making small changes or choosing ecofriendly alternatives (you'll see lots of them in this chapter). At its simplest

this could mean constructing a pond that needs no electrical pump, or the bigger commitment of building a garden with as little cement as possible (cement being one of the world's biggest polluters of carbon dioxide).

The sustainable garden need never compromise good design, either – look at the medal winners in contemporary flower shows as testament to this.

Opposite: Reclaimed materials give any garden a real time-worn, lived-in appearance. When used cleverly they also help create something unique.

Right, top: Many contemporary garden-makers embrace the opportunity to introduce diverse habitats or select plants such as stonecrop (*Sedum*) and coneflower (*Rudbeckia*) to attract beneficial predators.

Right: Urban gardens have become the guardians of fauna, and provide resting and nesting spots for wildlife as it travels across towns and cities. A simple bug box or berrying tree such as rowan (*Sorbus aucuparia*) can help immensely – big changes aren't essential.

Material matters

Materials selection is a key area of ecofriendly garden design. All garden materials impact on the environment, but some are clearly better than others. Compromises may be necessary, but they needn't have a drastic effect on your budget, the look you're after in the garden or how the space is to be used.

WHAT'S THE PROBLEM WITH PEAT?

Peat is partially decomposed plant material. For years it's been the main component in composts, taking over from the soil-based John Innes range developed in the 1930s. Peat is dug out of peat bogs, and this depletion causes irreparable damage to precious natural habitats. Peat forms very slowly – at about 1mm ($^1/_{24}$in) a year. Because machines can strip a peat layer of more than 23cm (9in) each year, harvesting peat simply isn't sustainable.

If you want to reduce your use of peat, stop using it as a mulch or soil conditioner. Ethics aside, there are good alternatives, like home-made compost and well-rotted farmyard manure, that perform just as well and contain higher levels of nutrients.

If you want to cut back on using peat in potting composts, buy peat-free or reduced-peat compost – it'll say so on the bag; for good quality, buy the best you can afford.

Points to consider

Energy costs are an obvious thing to think about when planning a garden. Just how much energy would be used in the extraction, manufacture and delivery of materials to your garden? Imported materials might cost less, but may have had a long journey using many fuel kilometres to get to you.

Recycled or reclaimed materials and character-packed curios are an easy way to up your green credentials, but shop around before you settle on anything.

Certified timber should be the first choice for your garden. Look for a stamp from the Programme for the Endorsement of Forest Certification (PEFC) or Forest Stewardship Council (FSC). This means that the wood has been cut from a sustainable source and is not from an area of uncontrolled illegal deforestation.

Installation

How a material is installed is important too. Concrete manufacture is a seriously polluting process, plus concrete itself is a major contributor to the unnatural urban heat island effect (see p11). Could dry-stone, cob,

Right: Wood is a favourite material of many designers (including me); just make sure it comes from a sustainable source.

rammed earth walls – even a dense hedge – work just as well? And loose materials like gravel, or clay pavers and bricks laid on compacted sand, are an ecofriendly alternative where solid paving isn't necessary. Being permeable these materials allow rainwater to soak away naturally too.

Also consider how a material behaves after installation and how it might be disposed of. Does maintenance necessitate the use of nasty chemicals? Does solid paving channel water to already overloaded storm drains? Can modern plastics be recycled easily?

A new aesthetic?

The sustainability cause has seen an upsurge in the use of renewable materials like green oak, hazel, plants (yes, plants!) and honest natural materials like stacked stone and gravel (although there are concerns about quarrying stone and dredging gravel). But there's no need to wear the ecotag as a straitjacket; instead use it to make informed choices. Continue to buy new materials and modern technologies (especially if they're more energy efficient); just consider their origin, manufacture and behaviour carefully, before doing so.

A new attitude

It's not just the way we design our gardens that's changed; the way we look after them has evolved too. Pesticide use is on the wane because of mounting concerns about its impact on bees and wildlife, and also on our food supply. Climate change affects the way we water the plants. Careful soil-management strategies like mulching to conserve soil moisture and the use of drought-tolerant plants are now common, to stave off possible water shortages. The adage 'right plant, right place' is being taken more seriously than ever before (see p105). Happy plants are healthy plants, needing less water and chemical support from fertilisers and pesticides.

This chapter now looks at key themes to consider in the modern urban garden. Most of these concern the way we live (or would like to!), but some respond to important issues such as the conservation of wildlife and biodiversity.

Below: There are many modern ecofriendly alternatives to traditional materials. These steps might look like concrete, but they're actually made from recycled CDs.

10 simple ways to a 'green' garden

1 Encourage wildlife

2 Avoid or limit the use of chemical pesticides and fertilisers

3 Choose the right plant for the right place

4 Garden organically

5 Make your own compost

6 Grow some fruit and vegetables

7 Avoid using peat

8 Manage water effectively and conserve it wherever possible

9 Mulch regularly

10 Reuse, recycle and buy recycled and reclaimed products

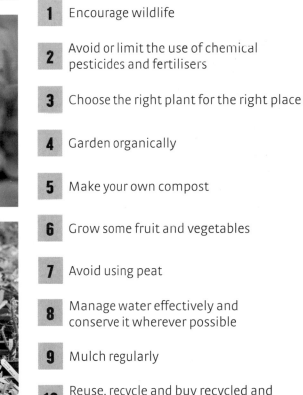

Top: Making your own compost is so simple and without doubt the simplest way to up your green credentials.

Centre, top: Using plants with open-faced flowers like coneflowers (*Echinacea*) and nectar-rich globe thistles (*Echinops*) encourages natural predators, so you can cut back on the chemicals.

Centre, bottom: Growing vegetables and fruit, especially those you've propagated yourself, is an easy and cheap way to cut your carbon footprint.

Bottom: Drought-tolerant plants, such as these cacti and succulents, ultimately take care of themselves and need very little water. Just make sure that you choose plants that are hardy – such as sempervivums and sedums – if you plan to grow them outdoors over winter.

Above: Bearing their size and 'lack of landscape' in mind, urban gardens should forge links with the architecture of the home, as the designer has done here.

Right: Bold architecture needs an equally brave response in the garden. Here, patterns in the building are instantly recognisable in the garden. Simplicity like this should always be cherished.

The urban 'style'

Urban gardens can show influences from many different styles and themes – formal, informal, cottage, tropical, modernist, to name a few – all mixed in a melting pot of creativity. Sustainability of course comes into it too. Almost anything goes, as most urban gardens aren't visually affected by surrounding scenery and so there's less need to blend a design into the neighbourhood beyond the boundary – front gardens, balconies and roof terraces with extensive views being obvious exceptions.

A less-is-more approach works best and subtle execution is important, especially if you have a familiar theme in mind. Try to capture the essence of the theme rather than create a pastiche of one or, worse still, two or more combined. For example, a full-blown Italian, Islamic or Japanese garden can look odd away from its natural home.

Forging links

An urban garden should connect visually with the home – particularly its architecture – which in turn will blur the boundaries between the two. To do this look at the proportions of doors and windows, the shapes in the façade, even the colour, and use these outside.

In order to blend house with garden, many designs feature a strong geometric, often rectilinear layout. This is a feature common to both classic formal design and modernist style. Clean lines are commonplace, whether the layout is symmetrical or asymmetrical.

Garden designs based on squares and/or rectangles forge a relationship and make good use of space. For a more dynamic design these might be orientated at an

angle along diagonal lines (30 degrees and 45 degrees being most usual), which can also make a garden feel bigger; the eye is drawn to the sides, not just the back.

When positioned centrally, circles and ovals are popular ways of focusing attention on the middle of a garden (to help distract from neighbouring eyesores, for example). They also work really well if the garden is viewed from above.

Gentle arcs create a more relaxed, organic look, and bring contrast to geometric shapes. Try to avoid fiddly curves, which are tricky to interpret, difficult to mow if in a lawn, or wasteful if you're cutting stone pavers to fit.

Larger suburban gardens can accommodate more informal designs, but even here the first third of the garden will usually reflect the architecture of the home, to form that all-important link.

Relaxed modern minimalism

This town garden by landscape architect Christopher Bradley-Hole features a simple but strong framework combined with gorgeous attention to detail – qualities essential in all garden designs. Although finished in 2004, the garden is as timeless as ever.

Underlining much of the designer's work is the modernist movement, characterised by clean lines, strong asymmetric geometry and an elegant architectural aesthetic. These characteristics work particularly well in urban gardens. Think of a Piet Mondrian painting or the buildings of Le Corbusier and Ludwig Mies van de Rohe and you'll get the idea.

An immediately 'readable' layout is important to all urban gardens but particularly so in modernist ones. Here, the design is underpinned with a bold rectilinear geometry (a characteristic common to modernist gardens) that also features strongly in the vertical elements – notably the fence, the Yorkstone benches and freestanding yew (*Taxus*) hedges. Not only do these reinforce the pattern but alongside the multistemmed shadbushes (*Amelanchier*) they create the necessary contrast to the horizontal elements, again a common trait in gardens of this style.

Clinical attention to detail is synonymous with the modernist garden, but it's a feature to be found in any

Above: Smooth-sawn wooden benches reinforce the geometry of this design, and importantly 'full stop' the space. They also have a real sculptural quality.

Right & Below: Dusky cranesbill (*Geranium phaeum* var. *phaeum* 'Samobor'), Martin's spurge (*Euphorbia* x *martini*) and pheasant's tail grass (*Anemanthele lessoniana*) – planted in gravel for textural contrast – remove any severity from the layout.

Above: Freestanding hedges and shadbushes help shelter and shade the terrace from the rest of the garden.

situation where strong geometry is present. Designers often edit out all superfluous details in favour of an honest simplicity. This approach is evidenced here from the minimal joint width in the Yorkstone paving to the crisp, back-to-basics nature of the bespoke timber fence and stone benches.

Gardens like this one might be pared back to their bare bones, but ornamental planting is still important for colour, texture and seasonal interest.

WHY THIS GARDEN WORKS

· Bold geometric layout with complementary materials that blend beautifully
· Clever division of space using planting and hedges
· Abundant, low-maintenance, drought-tolerant planting contrasts and softens the rectilinear geometry
· Generous-sized 'rooms' make the garden feel bigger than it actually is

'Planted' gardens

Plants are essential in all gardens but even more so in an urban environment surrounded by grey concrete. For some people, plants are the garden, of course, and they're grumpy if not knee deep in cuttings and compost all day long.

Urban planting style

Traditional urban gardens have often miniaturised the planting from their country or cottage cousins. But today a pared-down, low-maintenance palette is more common, with plants selected for both year-round and architectural interest. As Catherine Heatherington's garden on p64 shows, supporting wildlife is also an important consideration.

Where space is tight, designers also think about how plants might perform other design roles, such as privacy and screening, or how they might contribute to the garden's structure, by defining one space from another.

Spatial design with plants

In the home, walls and ceilings divide what would otherwise be an open-plan interior into a series of more intimate rooms, each one having a particular role and function, whether it's cooking, sleeping or work. On a practical level, without this delineation of space, it would be impossible to stop one activity impacting on the next. From a design perspective, walls and ceilings also help give spaces their own identity, plus they encourage curiosity (for example, what's around the corner?), create focused views from one room to the next, and determine the experience you have when walking through your home.

Plants in urban gardens can do the very same job, although no wall I know of can give off a beautiful scent! Plants are a lot cheaper too, even if you buy big for instant impact.

A plant paradise?

In this book you'll see many contemporary urban gardens that rely on a formal backbone of architectural evergreens, clipped hedges or topiary; these reinforce the layout and invite links to surrounding architecture.

However, some designers take exactly the opposite approach, by including extensive informal collections to soften hard edges or hide them completely.

Filling a garden with plants helps blur boundaries between one garden and the next, making your garden seem bigger. A plant-packed garden could also take you to another place entirely – a relaxed country cottage or jungle paradise.

Maintenance is certainly important to consider with the plant-packed approach, but even a garden brimming with plants shouldn't occupy too much time, if you choose with the characteristics of the space in mind.

Left: Note how this densely planted scheme complements the modern architecture of the building perfectly.

Below: To many people, the garden is the place to get a 'fix of green' – you'll get plenty of fix here!

CASE STUDY

A calm jungle courtyard

A contemporary formal style and an informal proliferation of plants are evident in this serene woodland jungle by landscape designer Tom Stuart-Smith. It shows that you can have the best of both worlds, even in a small space.

Key to the design brief was year-round interest, but the garden's clay soil (improved with grit and compost) and its partially shady conditions have also obviously been an influence.

Dramatic soft tree ferns (*Dicksonia antarctica*) dominate, adding height throughout, and the feathery fronds cast shade and shadow on the boundaries and plants below. Growing underneath are evergreen box (*Buxus*) (clipped into different-sized balls) and semi-evergreen Japanese forest grass (*Hakonechloa macra*), while snowdrops (*Galanthus*) feature for spring.

Immediately obvious is the lack of emphasis on colour; instead, form and texture come to the fore in the choice of plants and also in the hardwood cladding,

polished concrete terrace and crushed granite path. The path leads to a sandpit for the owners' young children.

With such a limited palette of plants, maintenance is kept to an absolute minimum. Only the box balls need trimming to retain their shape. The carpeting Japanese forest grass keeps weeds down. Even the exotic tree ferns won't require regular work. In warm sheltered gardens like this one they keep their leaves all year round and and won't need wrapping with fleece unless particularly cold temperatures are forecast.

Climbing hydrangeas (*Hydrangea anomala* subsp. *petiolaris*) have also been included, and these create attractive patterns on the crisp hardwood strips cladding each boundary.

Left: Repetition and the sheer scale of only a few plant species are what give this design such drama.

Below: Views from the house are important to consider in any garden design. A garden should entice you to go outside from every angle.

Above: Even though the planting is informal and abundant, it beautifully complements the strong geometry of the home.

WHY THIS GARDEN WORKS

· Sublime example of simplicity and restraint
· Functional, child-friendly design
· Careful juxtaposition of pattern, form and texture
· Pared-down collection of low-maintenance plants and materials, repeated to bring unity to the composition

Gardens for living in

The 'outdoor room' concept has been called many things over the years – the 'living room', the 'fifth room', the 'green room' – but the original idea pioneered by John Brookes and modernist designer Thomas Church is as relevant today as it ever was, especially in urban gardens.

Today we use urban gardens in every way imaginable, often for activities carried out primarily in the house, whether it's entertaining, sleeping, working, sometimes even watching TV!

A space to relax

It's likely you'll spend much of your time just sitting in the garden, so a generous dining area with a table and chairs – or just loungers where space is tight – is usually top priority. For ease of use this area is best sited close to the house. With enough space you can accommodate both formal and informal seating areas.

Furniture is a big design feature and an important part of an urban garden's structure; consider it early on in the design process. Your garden's style or theme will determine the materials, fabrics and finish.

Barbecues and ovens

Cooking outdoors on a warm afternoon can bring immeasurable pleasure. A simple portable barbecue is fine for most people, while outdoor ovens are also popular, especially if they have an overhead canopy enabling year-round use.

For rustic alfresco entertaining, a pizza oven is a cheaper option. These are usually made of prefabricated rendered concrete and come in kit form. Unless you're competent with a trowel, you might need a bricklayer to build a supporting structure.

Hot tubs and showers

Nowadays the hot tub is no longer exclusive to the rich and famous; smaller, one-person, cedar-clad models or plunge pools look good and fit more modest budgets. A cover to keep leaves out is essential, as well as a canopy if you want to use the tub in all weathers.

Cheaper than a hot tub is an outdoor shower. The easiest option is to build it against the kitchen or bathroom wall, where a plumber can run pipework through the wall. Privacy is necessary, so tiled walls or cheaper bamboo, heather or willow screens also need to be factored into the cost.

Cold-water showers are fine for hot days, but water from mains systems is always warmer. However, it can also be heated from solar panels or ground-source heat pumps to save on energy and environmental costs.

Opposite, top: 'Shed working' has never been more popular, but you'll need electricity, heating and, in particular, insulation. There are many specially designed outdoor offices available in kit form that can slot into the tiniest space. Most don't need planning permission.

Opposite, bottom: A sizeable dining area is important if you want to eat and entertain. Make it as large as possible.

Right: A small outdoor swimming pool is a wonderful luxury to have where there is space, especially for families. Hot tubs or plunge pools are suitable for more modest budgets.

Alfresco entertaining

Designed by Charlotte Rowe for two housemates in London, this garden is a stylish, functional outdoor room in the tradition of Australian and Californian gardens, where outdoor living is a way of life.

The garden features an ample dining area big enough to seat ten people in comfort, a bespoke, built-in outdoor kitchen in the most sheltered corner, and an informal lounge with comfy chairs to sit in and relax with friends.

The kitchen includes a shiny stainless-steel barbecue that runs off mains gas, enabling the owners to cook at the flick of a switch. Importantly, the whole cooking area blends in; built-in barbecues and outdoor kitchens must look good all the time, whether in use or not, especially in cool climates.

If you don't have space or the budget for a built-in cooking station, opt for cheaper portable grills – some of which boast hot plates, griddles and rotisseries. Those with wheels can be pushed out of sight when not in use.

Considered attention to detail is obvious in the design. Smooth-sawn, blue-black basalt makes up the main surface, complemented by ivory-coloured walls (the same colour used in the house) and giant limestone planks. Again, the same limestone is a feature throughout the ground floor, so using it outdoors

Above: Limestone planks bridge the pool that flows from the top tier down the steps to the bottom.

Right: Built-in cupboards clad with creamy grey limestone store the cooking paraphernalia.

Below: With a giant glass façade and repetition of materials, the transition between inside and outdoors Is almost seamless.

Above: For privacy, fastigiate hornbeams (*Carpinus betulus* 'Fastigiata') were planted to screen off the health club behind. Pruning to keep them at a proportionate size was factored in by the designer.

furthers the connection between indoors and out.

Human wants and needs take precedence over gardening in this garden, but clipped yew (*Taxus*) and box (*Buxus*) alongside low-maintenance perennials like *Geum* 'Prinses Juliana', *Achillea* 'Terracotta', *Salvia nemorosa* 'Caradonna', *Agapanthus* 'Enigma', Japanese forest grass (*Hakonechloa macra*) and Corsican hellebore (*Helleborus argutifolius*) have been included to 'green' the space.

WHY THIS GARDEN WORKS

· Spacious and versatile eating, entertaining, and rest and relaxation areas
· Bold details (*eg* the furniture, pots and water feature) reinforce the clean geometry of the design
· Easy-to-maintain planting provides privacy, greens the aesthetic and subtly softens hard lines

Hybrid spaces

Recent developments in glazing technology and insulation have meant the concept of an outdoor room has been taken to another level in the last 15 years. Many new buildings or extensions feature huge glass doors and windows, truly making the garden an integral part of the home.

A clear layout

Where there are expansive views onto the garden, a clear, easily identifiable layout is best – one that works visually not only from the ground floor but also from first and second floors if need be (another reason why strong, no-frills geometry is essential). The position of focal points to catch the eye, plus the density of plantings, should be considered from each door or window that overlooks the space.

Connections

The easiest way to create links and blur boundaries is to take a little of the inside of the house outside. Indoor furnishings could suggest the planting palette. Paint colours used inside might inspire similar colours on freestanding walls. Raised planting beds could even mirror the colour and height of kitchen cupboards. Lighting is particularly useful, with many effects inspired by interior or theatre design (for more on lighting, see p50).

Use of surface materials continued from the house into the garden is the most obvious unifying technique. But while some materials can be adopted indoors and out – frostproof slate, sandstone or travertine, for example – another material of a similar colour or size is usually employed outside, because a different surface finish is needed (for grip a slightly textured, 'picked' or 'riven' texture is essential) or a thicker material is required (although this does depend on the sub-base or foundation). Importantly, the chosen garden materials must cope with frost and wet conditions.

Even if you can use the same material outside as you do indoors, don't forget it will weather differently when exposed to the elements.

Above: Huge bifolding doors pull back to reveal a light and airy hybrid space. The same flooring completely blurs the boundaries between inside and outdoors.

Opposite: With a vista like this it's tricky to identify where the house ends and the garden begins!

Avoiding damp

A level surface between inside and outdoors creates a seamless transition, but to achieve this is not quite as simple as raising up an outside patio or terrace to the internal floor height; the damp-proof course (DPC) needs to be considered. If you breach it by building higher than the DPC, damp will set in – and fast. For new extensions a high DPC can be factored in on the drawing board; if not, channels filled with gravel and slot drains (also called interceptor drains) installed on the threshold between inside and out are possible solutions, but always consult a professional for this type of work.

Below: The paving here has been cut and laid so the joints between each slab draw the eye up and out into the garden, where the sculpture and yellow lounger beyond reward that visual journey.

CASE STUDY

A marriage of past and present

I love this design for its elegant simplicity. Although more than 10 years old, it's still a firm favourite with me. You might think a decade is a long time, and garden design has moved on significantly since then, but great design doesn't date – it's timeless.

This garden is owned by architect Rupert Wheeler and designed in collaboration with neighbour Paul Gazerwitz (of del Buono Gazerwitz Landscape Architecture). The courtyard was originally a covered workshop that Rupert removed to create a garden space. Vestiges of the workshop's former life were allowed to remain, in order to pay homage to the past. Most noticeable are the steel joists – the support structure for the old roof. These have a sculptural quality; they also help to frame views into the space and provide support for large climbing roses (*Rosa*).

The garden evokes a courtyard in Provence (an ambience much desired by the owners), and this is reflected in the choice of surface materials, and other design details like the seats and pots. That, and the shady aspect, were a big influence on the planting too, with white being the colour of choice to stand out at night. Voluptuous *Hydrangea arborescens* 'Annabelle', blousy *Rosa* 'Rambling Rector', fringed iris (*Iris japonica*) and self-seeding Mexican fleabane (*Erigeron karvinskianus*) add to the relaxed atmosphere. Glossy green arum lily (*Zantedeschia aethiopica*) and box (*Buxus*), along with a reflective pond that spills over into a tiny basement, also inject light into the shade.

What works so well is the relationship between the house and garden, seen from all angles. The materials – a subtle blend of modern and traditional – offer contrasting forms and textures.

Left: Good views of the planting and other features can be enjoyed through the glass façade on the ground floor.

Below: This garden looks fantastic from every angle, being designed like a picture.

Above: The sweeping handrail directs the eye into the space, while the box balls act as a visual pause to the main focal point – a Cretan urn at the back.

WHY THIS GARDEN WORKS

- Elegant abundant design with time-worn character
- Open spacious layout makes the most of limited space
- Restrained use of an inexpensive palette of sustainable ecofriendly materials
- Uninterrupted views throughout
- Complementary blend of modern and traditional design details

Above: Coloured neon and LED (light-emitting diode) strip lights are available, but most designers prefer simple and subtle soft white light.

Left: Lighting water is fun, and creates an ethereal ambience. Moving water throws shimmering patterns onto nearby surfaces, while still water reflects mirror images.

Night gardens

To realise the full potential of an urban garden you should be able to use it at night. Using night-scented plants and clever garden lighting, you can make the time you spend outdoors significantly more enjoyable.

Lighting can be decorative, functional or, ideally, both. Just keep it simple and question carefully where and why you're using it. There are many different fixtures and fittings and many effects worth considering – grazing, uplighting, spotlighting, downlighting, moonlighting, silhouetting and shadowing being the most common. But don't overdo it.

POWER SUPPLY

Garden lights either work through a transformer that provides a low-voltage current, or come directly from the mains supply. Both systems must be installed by an electrician, although some smaller, low-voltage sets can be fitted by amateurs once the power supply – usually a waterproof socket with a residual-current device (RCD) – has been fixed outside. Low-voltage lighting is easier to install, is safer and more flexible too, particularly if you leave long cable 'tails' attached to each light so that you can move them around when the fancy takes you.

Natural flame

Candles tick the ecofriendly box. Tea lights in glass jars, or church candles in hurricane lamps, are cheap and look gorgeous. Fire bowls or braziers are delightful too, bringing both light and warmth. They're also more environmentally friendly than gas-powered or mains-electric patio heaters. Choose one with a spark guard for use around children.

Neighbours and wildlife

Disruption to neighbours and wildlife must be considered. Moths, bats and owls become disorientated by artificial light; it can also dazzle animals. Lighting on a manually controlled, passive infrared sensor or programmable timer is best and saves energy. To stop glare, choose fittings with a hood or 'eyelid'.

Night scents

Many plants save their scent for evenings or after dark. Try moonflower (*Ipomoea alba*), evening primrose (*Oenothera*), night phlox (*Zaluzianskya capensis*), night-scented stocks (*Matthiola longipetala* subsp. *bicornis*) or star jasmine (*Trachelospermum jasminoides*). Moths will love them too.

Opposite: If a roaring natural outdoor fire like this doesn't entice the family and any visitors outside, then nothing will!

CASE STUDY

The light fantastic

This garden assumes an otherworldly appearance at night.
It's a stylish but functional outdoor room, because entertaining –
particularly in the evening – was at the top of the owner's wish
list to designer Claire Mee.

The various lighting effects are designed to maximise
all the views from the house, even in winter. 'At this
time it's still – like a painting,' Claire says.

Tall planted pots opposite the kitchen window are
a key sculptural element; at night they're discreetly
uplit from flat spots installed in the ipe decking
below. (I love uplighting clipped topiary and trees too,

especially those with shaggy or peeling bark like river
birch/*Betula nigra*).

A spotlight at the base of a brick or stone wall
presents a wonderful lighting opportunity, as the light
grazes over the surface, throwing the texture into
sharp relief. Here the designer 'washes' the sculptural
COR-TEN steel panels with light to create a warm

Right: Although evening entertaining topped the client's brief, the design still works well during the day.

WHY THIS GARDEN WORKS

- Uses focused design layout
- Subtle yet appealing lighting techniques define the layout at night
- Reveals careful appreciation of those design details that work best when lit up
- Uses clean and comfortable materials, ideal for alfresco entertaining
- Bold but low-maintenance plant palette

Above: The entire installation is controlled by a programmable panel, with lights on different circuits. This enables the owners to create different effects, but the whole lot can be timed to switch off when not in use.

Right: Different lighting effects combine to create a wonderful ambience after dark.

fiery glow and pick out the subtle rusty texture. With a downlight fixed to the wall higher up, the opposite pattern could have been created.

Lit from the rear, the bamboo is thrown into silhouette, but with the blank wall behind, shadowing would work just as well. With a spotlight positioned in front of architectural evergreens like agave and phormium, the surface behind acts like a projector screen reflecting ghostly shadows.

Claire designs her own lighting schemes, but like all experienced garden designers uses a qualified electrician for advice and installation. While some low-voltage systems are suitable for home installation, a professional is essential for anything ambitious.

Family-friendly gardens

The family-friendly urban garden has to be all things to all people, so flexibility is essential. Always avoid creating a garden specifically with children in mind. It'll date quickly as their ages and interests move on. Focus instead on having generous-sized, multifunctional areas that everyone can use, whether for work, rest or play.

Left: Safety and security are paramount. Here, smooth decking, artificial turf and deep planting beds (without sharp corners) keep children away from the edge, making this big balcony a safe place to play for primary schoolchildren.

Below: What a brilliant solution to family living! Parents can monitor what's going on, while children still have freedom to explore, safely. The sandpit can be easily (and cheaply) changed as the children grow.

Space for living

The patio or terrace sometimes has to accommodate dining furniture, barbecue and train set, all at the same time, so try to make it as big as possible. Smooth paving or decking is the best surface, being hardwearing, comfortable and 'wheel'-friendly too.

A lawn will satisfy the whole family. However, grass quickly shows signs of wear and you can't use it all year round. Permeable artificial turf might be a better option in these circumstances (see p139).

A designated play area will delight, and importantly keep toys in their place. Try and subtly screen it with lacy planting, slatted screens or freestanding trellis. Children can then indulge their imagination, apparently in secret, but you can still keep an eye on their play times. Even in tiny gardens there's often room for a cleverly designed sandpit (with cover) or a swing slung from a tree or sturdy pergola.

Water

Children of all ages love water, but safety is vitally important. For youngsters, waterfalls, spouts or bubble fountains with a hidden underground reservoir are best. For older children a wildlife pond can provide entertainment for hours, but, if toddlers are around, cover it with special metal or plastic grilles that can be retrofitted and hidden just under the surface.

Suitably tough plants

Plants in family gardens should be easy to look after and tough enough to withstand being whacked by a football. Architectural evergreens, wildlife-friendly shrubs, ornamental grasses and sturdy perennials like yarrow (*Achillea*) are perfect. Obviously avoid thorny, poisonous or irritant plants.

Grow-their-own

Children love to grow their own fruit and vegetables, and most like eating the results! Try and give them their own patch – even a half-barrel will do. Make sure it's in a sunny, easy-to-dig spot that won't be a struggle to get going. Invest in fast flowers and veg – children are impatient! Radishes, salad leaves and pot marigolds (*Calendula*) should be ready in only six weeks. Strawberries are always a hit.

Top: Wooden play equipment blends well in a small garden and won't scream for attention, whereas plastic sets can prove an ugly addition.

Above: Give children a couple of big boulders, a sloping bank or a simple set of stepping stones such as this, and they'll make up their own games for hours on end.

Fun for all the family

This contemporary family garden ticks all the wish-list boxes – and more. Stuart Craine created it for a family with young children, and cleverly divided the space into three different rooms, each subtly screened from the other.

Together, the giant glass doors and decked terrace help blur the boundary between inside and out – a key part of the brief requested by Stuart's South African clients. Here, the raised beds usefully double up as seats (or places to jump from) and a shimmering water wall is cleverly positioned (see image, opposite top) to draw the eye out from inside the house.

Eating outside as a family was important to the client, so the garden features a generous seating and barbecue area. This is sunken into the ground, revealing more vertical planes and in turn making the whole garden feel bigger. The chunky, oak-and-steel-braid pergola, dripping with fragrant chocolate vine (*Akebia*) and star jasmine (*Trachelospermum jasminoides*), adds height

Right: A clever layout means you can't see the whole design all at once, making the journey through the garden much more exciting.

WHY THIS GARDEN WORKS

· Flexible multipurpose design, with interconnecting 'rooms' for different family activities
· Robust, child-friendly planting with year-round interest
· Stylish yet safe design details, such as a toughened glass balustrade surrounding the basement steps
· Functional play area made of visually sympathetic materials

Above: 'The client wanted a stylish, visually exciting space, but one that would allow the children to play safely, unsupervised,' says Stuart Craine, the designer.

Right: This structure blends in and doesn't visually dominate the garden, unlike bright kit-form apparatus and play equipment.

and offers privacy from neighbouring gardens, but it's also there to offer shade from the hot sun – essential for the young children in the family.

Next door is the children's zone; this features a wooden climbing frame, swing and monkey bars built into a den-cum-playhouse-cum-storage shed, partially disguised with a green roof. Designated play areas should have a soft surface; here, Stuart uses artificial turf that never gets muddy. Play bark or shredded rubber (avoid bright colours) would also work well.

Key to the planting brief was year-round interest, so lush but robust plantings of bamboo iris (*Iris confusa*), *Agapanthus* 'Albus', loquat (*Eriobotrya japonica*) and bamboo envelop each space.

Productive gardens

Even though there might not be room for a large vegetable patch in your urban garden, you'll be amazed at what you can grow there. A few large tubs can yield handfuls of fresh pickings (see p166).

The potager

While functionality is at the heart of the productive garden, appearance also counts. Medieval monks in monastic gardens thought so, as did the French, who created the formal potager – an ornamental vegetable garden where crops were planted alongside attractive perennials, roses (*Rosa*) and clipped topiary.

Still popular today, the full-blown potager or Victorian kitchen garden is usually a luxury where space is tight, and it needs quite a bit of work. However,

you can still style the garden in a similar way, using woven-willow supports, ornate arches and weathered terracotta. Or bring the look bang up to date, by combining these materials with steel braid, zinc and polished oak.

To enhance the strong geometrical layout, rows of lavender (*Lavandula*) and rosemary (*Rosmarinus*) alongside paths are popular and will also attract beneficial pollinators and hoverflies, whose larvae prey on aphids.

Attractive edibles

Where space is tight it is possible to mingle attractive crops within beds and borders – a more relaxed approach but still following the potager or kitchen garden tradition. Tall sweetcorn, fennel and globe artichokes are back-of-the-border favourites. Shrubs can be replaced with black currants or gooseberries. Blue-grey, early autumn leeks like 'King Richard' perfectly complement frothy pink *Geranium* 'Mavis Simpson', smaller *Sedum* 'Bertram Anderson' and *Nepeta racemosa* 'Walker's Low'. Given a rich fertile soil and a sunny spot, even the humble potato has something to offer.

Pretty climbing vegetables can be used on walls and fences. Runner beans won't mind cool walls. In sunnier spots grow climbing French beans like 'Goldfield' (yellow pods) or 'Empress' (dark blue pods).

As crops are harvested, gaps in the bed or border are inevitable, so plan for another crop (preferably a different one) straight afterwards. Alternatively, let ornamental perennials take over, or plug the gaps with some seasonal bedding or a few fast-growing hardy annuals like love-in-a-mist (*Nigella*) instead.

Above: Maximise your plot's cropping potential by training pretty edible climbers (here, grapes) overhead, or up a wall or fence.

Left: Raised beds warm up quickly in spring (useful for early sowings), and it's possible to grow tasty crops – no matter how poor the soil might be underneath. Designers use raised beds to divide one area from another too.

Edible elegance

A practical productive garden can still be very beautiful, as this modern elegant oasis by del Buono Gazerwitz Landscape Architecture goes to show. Its formal unfussy framework is a feature common to the designer's work.

Strong structure is important in urban gardens. Here, yew (*Taxus*) hedging, pleached hornbeams (*Carpinus*) and flat, umbrella-trained mulberries (*Morus*) form the backbone of the garden. These help to define space, yet together with large natural trellis screens they offer privacy from surrounding buildings – a very important stipulation from the clients.

The mulberries are the garden's most striking feature. They 'ceiling' the dining area, offering both privacy and shade from strong sun; however, they don't block it out completely. Furthermore, they also frame views in the garden and reinforce its formal layout overhead.

Plentiful plantings of iris, *Erysimum* 'Bowles's Mauve' and cranesbills (*Geranium*) feature throughout

Right: Pleached hornbeams with trellis behind create privacy and hide ugly eyesores.

WHY THIS GARDEN WORKS

- Elegant, formal, classic design with complementary design details
- Clean, clutter-free layout makes great use of space and builds a relationship with the surrounding architecture
- Immaculate design detailing using traditional ecofriendly materials and plants
- Abundant, colourful, wildlife-friendly planting includes attractive edibles

Above: Fruit trees and dining areas generally don't mix well as the fruit attracts wasps and stains surfaces. However, *Morus platanifolia*, the non fruiting, plane-leaved mulberry, has been used here, so such problems will not occur.

Right: As the designer Tommaso del Bueno explains, 'This is a garden for keen gardeners, who wanted variety, wanted a challenge; who longed for a "proper" garden. They are very keen cooks too.'

and help soften the scheme. Herb-filled, woven-willow raised beds are situated within easy reach of the house. These satisfy the need for growing productive plants but can easily accommodate fruit and vegetables if required.

Herbs have long been appreciated for their looks, and the herb garden in its full glory really is a feature to treasure. Purple sage (*Salvia officinalis* 'Purpurascens'), rosemary (*Rosmarinus officinalis*), chives (*Allium schoenoprasum*), lemon balm (*Melissa officinalis*), pineapple mint (*Mentha suaveolens* 'Variegata'), pennyroyal (*Mentha pulegium*) and lemon-scented thyme (*Thymus* x *citriodorus*) are effortlessly beautiful. They're also good, easily grown alternatives to traditional ground cover – such useful plants that really do look good... enough to eat!

Wildlife gardens

Urban gardens aren't just for our pleasure; they're essential for urban wildlife and also help to safeguard biodiversity. Encouraging wildlife into your garden makes it more entertaining too, especially for children.

No matter the style or theme of your garden, a few simple steps can yield big benefits for wildlife.

Plant power

Plants are essential to attract wildlife, but you don't have to use native plants exclusively. Just avoid highly bred cultivars with big blowsy or double flowers, most of which contain little or no pollen or nectar.

Lavender (*Lavandula*), fennel (*Foeniculum*), red valerian (*Centranthus ruber*), Michaelmas daisies (*Aster*) and golden rod (*Solidago*) attract bees, butterflies and hoverflies – Mother Nature's own pest control. Importantly, all are long-lasting. The berries of cotoneaster, mahonia and holly (*Ilex*) are all loved by birds. Hedges and climbers (especially ivy/*Hedera*) make perfect camouflaged nesting sites.

Trees also provide food and shelter for many different birds, animals and insects. In tiny gardens a 'pleached' or trained version might fit the space perfectly, if there is no room for a spreading tree.

Just add water

A pond attracts wildlife like nothing else, being a magnet for newts, frogs, dragonflies, birds and mammals. Just make sure you allow plenty of space for planting around the edge, so animals and insects can find protection and shelter. At least one sloping side is essential for visitors to get in and out easily. Deep-water plants and marginals such as flowering rush (*Butomus umbellatus*) planted in the boggy fringes provide both food and refuge for pond life.

To make good use of space in smaller gardens, integrate wildlife pools with other features such as a decking platform cantilevered out over the pool.

Right: While leaving piles of foliage and dead wood untouched, or letting the grass grow long, certainly helps, you don't need to compromise on appearances when creating a wildlife-friendly garden.

Above: A pond means wildlife, but it doesn't have to be an informal shape. Square, circular or rectangular ponds, which are more suitable for modern designs, work just as well.

SIMPLE WAYS TO ATTRACT WILDLIFE

Put up nesting boxes; some come with a video camera so you can watch bird behaviour.

Provide a wide variety of food. Song thrushes love dried fruit. Blackbirds adore rotten apples. Sunflower seeds attract chaffinches, goldfinches, blue tits and many other species.

Make compost. You'll encourage thousands of insects, beetles and slugs – a feast for foraging birds and hedgehogs.

Special bug boxes provide a home for hibernating lacewings and ladybirds – both control aphids.

Leave piles of foliage around the garden, for nesting hedgehogs. The hollow stems of perennials left uncut over winter will shelter hibernating insects.

Make a small wood pile (*eg* behind a shed); slug-eating slowworms and stag beetles love these conditions. Piles of stones are also a good habitat for slowworms and frogs.

Cut back on synthetic chemicals. Pesticides don't discriminate; they kill both beneficial wildlife and pests, so try to avoid using them wherever possible. Never buy slug pellets containing metaldehyde, which is also toxic to cats and dogs.

Control cats. Attaching a bell or, even better, two bells to a cat's collar could warn wildlife of imminent danger. If a neighbour's cat is problematic, try sprinkling eucalyptus oil, chilli pepper or lion dung over the soil (buy from garden centres); it may humanely deter over-eager foxes too.

Where nature meets design

'My garden is for people and wildlife,' says garden designer Catherine Heatherington, describing her own suburban haven. Here is a perfect example of how nature and people can live happily side by side in the same space.

With its visually strong layout and contemporary details such as a bold steel pergola and crisp-sawn Purbeck stone, this garden shows that modern designs can be wildlife-friendly too.

The rectangular pond is a big feature. Levels for different pond plants have been created throughout and the whole pond is lined with fibreglass to make it watertight. Stones and plants like marsh marigold (*Caltha palustris*) attract and shelter pond dwellers.

Catherine's planting exhibits careful appreciation of naturalistic principles. Plants are chosen to support those around them, be it as props to keep one another upright or to smother the soil and keep weeds at bay. Catherine explains, 'There are layers to the planting, from carpeting

Right: This wildlife-friendly garden features many contemporary design details such as a steel pergola.

WHY THIS GARDEN WORKS

- Contemporary design suitable for both people and wildlife
- Green roof, nectar-rich plants and a deep pool surrounded with plants all attract a variety of mammals, invertebrates and birds
- Strong structure and use of low-maintenance planting
- Careful appreciation of the patterns found in natural plant communities

Above: 'Just because it's a wildlife-friendly garden doesn't mean that a strong structure isn't important,' says Catherine.

Right: Although there are personal favourites like *Iris* 'Sable', *I.* 'English Cottage', *I.* 'Kent Pride' and *Allium hollandicum* 'Purple Sensation' plus bamboo (for a designer statement), most of the plants were chosen with wildlife in mind, to provide food or shelter.

ground cover right up to the larger trees, which provide numerous different habitats, exactly like you find in nature.' This approach supports wildlife, while planting self-sustaining groups reduces maintenance time.

Throughout the garden Catherine has included plants that provide nectar and pollen in lean but key times, with lungwort (*Pulmonaria*) and hellebores (*Helleborus*) for early spring, stonecrop (*Sedum*) and aster for late autumn. The semi-intensive, green roof atop the shed is a magnet for wildlife. Willow-leaved loosestrife (*Lysimachia ephemerum*) and purple fennel (*Foeniculum vulgare* 'Purpureum') attract hoverflies; Turkish sage (*Phlomis russeliana*) is beloved of bees; and berrying trees like sorbus and shadbush (*Amelanchier*) are for the birds.

SPACES AND PLACES

This chapter delves into the design and planting of specific urban spaces. But before that, a quick word about money, and how to make the most of it. I'm often asked the question 'Can a garden designer *really* make a difference?' In my experience the answer has got to be 'yes', particularly for difficult and sloping gardens.

Good designers will ascertain what would work, specify complicated hardscape connections and can manage the entire project. But a full design service in a small urban garden with a tight budget leaves little money for materials and plants. Given this, why not do your own design? A bit of research is essential, but you can always book a day's consultancy to help you initially.

Some things to consider

- Wholesale change is expensive. Could the addition of a simple focal point or a planting redesign be enough to transform the space?
- Invest in retaining structures, boundaries, patios and paths first. These form the garden's framework.
- Labour accounts for a significant portion of any budget. Local labour using local materials is cheaper (and more sustainable). You can do clearance work and planting yourself, but know your limits – plastering, brickwork and paving need an expert.
- The costs of sloping sites can really soar, with money going where you can't see it – on earthworks,

foundations and drainage. Wherever possible work with a slope to minimise expenditure and impact on the site. It's usually not necessary to terrace the whole space; one or two level areas are often enough. Decking is useful as it's built on top of, rather than into, a slope.
- Tight curves and complicated shapes are tricky to build unless they're of 'fluid' materials like gravel.
- Favour plants over hard landscaping as they cost less and are better for the environment: use hedges rather than walls, for example.
- Recycled materials are typically cheaper than new ones, and generally have a lower carbon footprint.
- Bespoke or commissioned elements, particularly intricate water features, are inevitably expensive.
- Small plants establish more readily and are cheaper than larger ones, but the latter are great for a sense of maturity. Trees for privacy, structural shrubs, topiary and hedges for security are all worth the higher cost; large perennials, ferns, climbers and grasses aren't – small plants reach a similar size in no time.

Opposite: Designs where plants feature prominently always cost significantly less than those full of hard landscaping.

Right: A lawn is the cheapest surfacing option by far. Seed for a new lawn costs less than rolls of precut turf, but it does need more care and attention initially.

Courtyards

A private, climber-cloaked, scent-soaked courtyard is revered in towns and cities everywhere. In this book I'm using the term rather loosely; because of their shape and size, many urban back gardens share identical characteristics with courtyards. Garden-makers therefore often treat them as one and the same.

The patio or terrace is the most important area of a courtyard garden – you could say any garden – as it serves numerous roles and functions. But two needs usually top the list: eating and entertaining.

Assessing your furniture options

Always allow enough space for eating outdoors. Thinking about the dining-room arrangement inside the house will help get the proportions right in your garden. If planning a new patio from scratch it might help to make flat, life-sized cardboard templates of a dining set, and then shuffle them about *in situ* to check the area is big enough. Consider this trick when buying new furniture for an existing terrace too.

As a guide, place the front of the chair at the edge of the table and then allocate another 75cm (30in) behind for manoeuvring the chair. To sit four people around a standard round table, 90–110cm (2³⁄₄–3¹⁄₂ft) wide, allow an area of 12–13sq m (130–140sq ft) for comfort; 9–10sq m (97–107sq ft) is a tight fit. Allow an area of 16–17sq m (172–183sq ft) to seat six around a round table 1.35m (4¹⁄₂ft) wide.

In a small garden, the chances are you won't have room for both formal dining furniture and informal loungers. Informal seating is a better choice if both indoor and outdoor dining sets will end up in close proximity to one another.

Space savers

Rectangular tables make the best use of space. Chairs without armrests and benches (which can be tucked underneath) allow more people to squeeze in. Collapsible or stackable furniture is also useful.

Built-in seats also make good use of space and can be combined with the construction of raised beds or retaining walls to spread the cost. Wood is best for the

Above: A dining area needs space to work as intended. Therefore in a small courtyard it's likely the whole garden will be orientated and designed with this activity in mind.

seat itself; it's warmer and more comfortable to sit on. Size-wise, the seat should be a minimum of 40cm (16in) and a maximum of 55cm (22in) high. For most people the ideal depth for a chair is 48–50cm (19–20in).

Balancing the design

To get a decent dining space and keep the garden as useable as possible might mean surfacing the whole area, restricting planting to the boundaries or to containers. However, thin strips around the perimeter are awkward to plant with anything but a few climbers or thin bamboos and grasses. Try to be as generous as possible; a larger border on one side only, balanced by container plantings on the other side, would mean there's scope for deeper, more imaginative planting.

Materials

Choose materials that complement the style of the house and garden, but don't use too many. Look at any garden

Below: Think vertically: in courtyards every boundary can be utilised for planting – making for a much more exciting and varied view than a blank wall or fence.

Bottom: Built-in benches make great use of space. Here the wooden top appears to float on the foliage below.

Right: Complemented by the plants around it, this partially hidden sculpture would be a lovely surprise when anyone is wandering through the garden.

in this book and you'll find they all feature no more than three or four different materials, adding perhaps another one as a special design detail or focal point.

Paving is the biggest feature (and typically the costliest) in a garden. Break up any large areas with smaller units of something else – granite 'planks' with a strip of square setts, for example – as too much of one thing looks monotonous. Alternatively, find another material that complements: for example, permeable flint gravel alongside porphyry pavers.

Focal point

All gardens, especially courtyards with inherent symmetry or designs with strong geometry, need a focal point to arrest the eye and 'anchor' the space.

A focal point can help to reinforce or dictate a garden's style or theme. Traditional sculptures are suitable for classic designs, while agricultural *objets d'art* complement cottage-style gardens; abstract artworks go best in modern-styled gardens.

Almost anything will do – a statue, water feature, three pots on parade. Just make sure the focal point will stand out against its surroundings (to determine the right size and shape see p76).

PRACTICAL MATTERS

Boundaries: The smaller the garden, the more important it is that the boundaries are well designed. Either hide them or make a feature out of them (more on this on p84).

Aspect: Make sure you choose the right plants for the right aspect of your courtyard. The microclimates alongside its north-, south-, east- and west-facing boundaries will differ.

Storage: A shed in a small courtyard is an eyesore. Screen it with climbers, freestanding trellis or evergreen shrubs. Painting it green and installing a 'living' roof (see p144) will camouflage it further.

Opposite, top: With its contrasting form to the rest of the composition, the boulder water feature makes an effective focal point and is perfectly at home in this seminaturalistic setting.

Opposite, bottom: The careful selection of a limited number of materials in this garden prevents it from becoming too cluttered, and also forges suitable links to the home.

Right: A metal sculpture, framed by the archway covered with climbers, rewards the eye and acts as a necessary 'full stop' to the design.

Urban oasis

Designer Declan Buckley created this garden for a large family.
It is a masterclass in modern urban garden design.

Outdoor entertaining was a key part of the brief from the client to this designer. So guests wouldn't sizzle in the sun, Declan assigned the dining area – big enough to accommodate eight people or more – to the shaded, north-facing corner by the house, which also offers protection from prevailing winds. Because of its positioning, and its flush threshold between inside and outdoors, it's ideal for alfresco entertaining.

The furniture is both a key design feature and a focal point – a characteristic common to urban gardens. It is a good idea to buy a set to last and one that complements your garden's style or theme; I find wood works everywhere (especially when it weathers). Obviously comfort is essential too. If storage space is limited choose materials like steel, aluminium or plastic, as Declan has done here, which can be cleaned quickly and left outdoors all year round.

A generous planting bed divides the dining area from informal seating in the back corner; here a parasol was included to provide shade. A tree could perform the same function, as well as shelter and overhead privacy.

The informal planting provides year-round interest. *Verbena bonariensis*, *Ammi majus*, *Foeniculum vulgare* 'Giant Bronze', *Calamintha nepeta* subsp. *nepeta*

Above: A simple change of level makes the journey though any garden much more exciting.

Right: The glass façade to this building has blurred completely the boundary between house and garden.

Below: Being light and lacy, the planting allows for glimpses of what lies beyond.

Above: Backed by abundant planting, this formal seating area is the perfect place to eat and entertain with friends and family.

'Blue Cloud' alongside grasses like *Miscanthus sinensis* 'Emmanuel Lepage' also contrast with the strong lines of the design.

Breaking up a small garden with planting creates intrigue and interest. But you might not have room to do this on the scale Declan has done here. Instead a line of tall pots spilling with grasses, or overhead beams covered with climbers – even a low raised bed – will help subtly separate one space from another.

WHY THIS COURTYARD GARDEN WORKS

- Crisp layout complements the geometry of the house and surrounding area
- Close attention to the boundaries: painted and clothed with suitable climbers
- Large living space positioned for shelter and privacy from neighbouring buildings
- Harmonious palette of wildlife-friendly plants that complement the hardscape and don't make the space feel hemmed in

Placing and choosing a focal point

To ensure a focal-point feature is the right size in relation to its surroundings, it should meet the conditions of the classic golden ratio. However, garden-makers usually make a more personal decision; when the focal point simply looks and feels right, it is right!

To gauge the size of a proposed focal point you can sketch out different ideas to scale on paper, or draw over photographs. I find it really helps to work *in situ* by stacking cardboard boxes on top of each other to get some idea of how the points of interest might look. This exercise is useful whether you've already got a feature in mind, or you simply want to determine what size and shape would work best.

1 Collect together boxes of different sizes and shapes; the bigger, the better. Given the choice, plain ones are better than those with lots of writing on them, being less distracting.

2 Position a box in the allocated space, and note how it looks. Is it too small, too big; is it too wide or too tall? Add more boxes to the first, or try smaller ones if it doesn't look right. Check the focal point from various positions around the garden and also from the house.

3   Having drawn attention to a particular view, does the planting on each side need improving? Also, take the background into account. It helps to take photographs as you go, which you can then reflect on later. Use a long ruler or a broom handle in each photo to put the size of the arrangement in context.

Below: In garden designs featuring strong symmetry like this one, an appropriately sized focal point is particularly important to reward the eye and 'full stop' the view.

4   Keep adding or subtracting boxes in different configurations until you find a combination that's the right height and width for the space. Record the measurements and choose a focal point with similar dimensions.

Front gardens

A front garden that is well designed and maintained brings pleasure not only to the owners but also to the entire neighbourhood. Being a public space, front gardens say a lot about the householders too. First impressions count!

Clear and easy access

Paths should be wide, obvious and fairly direct to the front door, otherwise it's tempting for visitors to cut corners, trampling plants in the process. Containers or climbers grown over the door will frame the entrance.

A firm footing is essential on a path, especially if it is in shade, so choose stable surface materials with a textured finish for grip. Link materials to the architecture of the home to forge a connection. This also applies to gates and any boundary treatments.

Car vs. garden

The benefits of vegetated front gardens and the problems associated with uncontrolled paving of these areas have now been recognised in many countries. Paved areas of more than a certain size may therefore now be subject to planning rules and regulations.

A combination of materials – paved paths for people, gravel for the car, for example – will control where a car parks. Heavy containers (which can't be easily stolen) or above-knee-height planting (which can be seen when reversing) will further delineate the area.

Permeable paving

Gardens that are covered with hardscape look ugly. Worst of all, they contribute to localised flooding; storms drains simply can't cope with all the run-off.

To tackle water run-off at source, use permeable paving – a sustainable urban drainage system (SUDS, for short) – which allows water to soak into the ground where it falls. There are many different permeable surfaces available: concrete block pavers (where water

Right: You can be creative and stand out from the crowd in both your front and back gardens, as here with these bird sculptures.

Above, left: These slip-resistant, clay pavers have been laid at an angle, to make the path feel wider and easy to navigate. The impassable planting either side means visitors will keep to the pre-determined route.

Above, right: A traditional palette of plants here includes box (*Buxus*), marguerites (*Leucanthemum vulgare*), Scotch thistle (*Onopordum acanthium*) and lady's mantle (*Alchemilla*).

Left: A lawn is pointless in a small front garden; instead fill the space with a riot of colourful perennials like lupins (*Lupinus*), cranesbill (*Geranium*) and Granny's bonnet (*Aquilegia vulgaris*).

can drain through the joints) is the most popular. Brown and grey 'rumbled' types look more natural.

Permeable gravel is a cheaper alternative, and the added crunch factor is useful for security. You can grow plants in it too. Gravel drives need solid foundations, which are best done by an experienced landscape contractor. A small section of paving at the threshold of house and garden will stop the gravel being dragged indoors. If loose gravel isn't appealing, choose permeable resin-bound gravel instead.

Year-round interest

Plants for front gardens need to be reliable, low-maintenance and offer year-round interest. Tidy shrubs such as *Pittosporum tobira* 'Nanum', *Elaeagnus* 'Quicksilver', *Euphorbia characias* subsp. *wulfenii*, rock rose (*Cistus* x *hybridus*) and *Viburnum tinus* 'Gwenllian' are ideal. Tough border conifers are useful too. Partner these with roses (*Rosa*), grasses and ground cover if there's room. Blue columnar *Juniperus communis* 'Hibernica' goes well with small white shrub roses,

lavender (*Lavandula*), mauve meadow rue (*Thalictrum*) and purple cultivars of *Iris sibirica*.

Fiery *Thuja occidentalis* 'Rheingold', pheasant's tail grass (*Anemanthele lessoniana*), *Helenium* 'Sahin's Early Flowerer', with *Crocosmia* x *crocosmiiflora* 'Emily McKenzie' and golden thyme (*Thymus*) in front will look good throughout the summer.

A front garden completely given over to parking can still accommodate attractive planting in the unused corners. Here, use half-barrels or big tubs. Think

vertically too; every boundary can be clothed in fragrant climbers like *Stauntonia hexaphylla* and *Clematis armandii* for sun, chocolate vine (*Akebia quinata*) and *Rosa* 'Albéric Barbier' for shade.

A big driveway – even one made using permeable paving – looks boring, so consider greening the strip under the car with low-growing ground cover like waldsteinia and creeping thyme. If the car isn't used daily, try shade-tolerant barrenwort (*Epimedium*) and periwinkle (*Vinca*) instead.

PRACTICAL MATTERS

Storage: Refuse bins and recycling boxes are an ugly necessity. A purpose-built bin store keeps everything neat and tidy. Paint it to match the house or camouflage it with ivy (*Hedera*) and a 'living' roof (see p144).

Security: Front doors or windows hidden from the street present an opportunity for burglars. Certainly include lots of plants, but avoid planting big specimens close to the house.

Lighting: Street lamps are often enough to illuminate most front gardens, but in darker streets additional bollards or surface-level spotlights drawing attention to paths or parking spaces are useful at steps or changes of level, for extra safety. Infrared-triggered spotlights enhance security; make sure you use one that has a timer, to save energy.

Rules and regulations: The amount of impermeable paving and the design of some front gardens is strictly controlled by law or local covenants that determine what you can and can't do. Check with your local authority.

Left: Formal topiary works wonderfully in front gardens. On this scale it might be too much to maintain for most people, so instead consider a few pots or a low hedge bordering the main path for emphasis.

Below: For the bins or bikes use a lockable store (painted the same colour as the front door) to help keep your garden neat and tidy.

CASE STUDY

Formality out front

'With front gardens often devoted to parking it's rare now to see a new front garden like this in London,' says designer Charlotte Rowe. 'Fortunately the client realised they only needed one parking space.' Plus, 'They specifically wanted a lawn.'

Topiary and the front garden are made for each other. Here, box (*Buxus*) balls spaced equidistant in a triangular pattern create a sculptural feature and further augment the garden's clean and crisp formality. Other plantings are restricted to white and green.

Pittosporum tenuifolium 'Irene Patterson', *Hydrangea arborescens* 'Annabelle', white ornamental onions (*Allium*) and iris feature in the surrounding borders. A hedge of tidy Portugal laurel (*Prunus lusitanica*) surrounds the garden. For more privacy *Betula utilis* var. *jacquemontii* trees were planted on the front boundary in front of the hedge. Although these will mature quickly, tree surgery to restrict their size was factored into the maintenance costs of the design.

Right: Clipped balls of sweet bay (*Laurus nobilis*) in gun-metal-coloured zinc containers emphasise the entrance to the home and welcome all arrivals.

WHY THIS FRONT GARDEN WORKS

- Strong layout complements the architecture of the home
- Clear division of 'car space' from 'garden space'
- Reliable, low-maintenance planting with year-round interest
- Trees and hedges provide privacy but don't cut out light or hide the home, enabling burglars to act unnoticed
- Careful design for rainwater run-off

Above: A sea of lady's mantle (*Alchemilla mollis*) divides the lawn from the parking area and helps to 'control' the position of the car.

Right: Box balls planted like this might make mowing a little tricky, but maintenance is kept to a minimum elsewhere.

Some front gardens are too small to warrant grass (permeable gravel being a better low-maintenance and environmentally friendly choice). But here it works and doesn't feel like a token gesture. A band of gravel around the edge emphasises the shape.

Sawn Yorkstone is used to surface the parking space-cum-path. Although this is not permeable it was carefully laid at a slight angle so that rainwater runs into the lawn, where it will be absorbed, and not out into the street. Yorkstone isn't cheap and being a light colour probably isn't a good choice for a classic car enthusiast (those oil stains!). However, it was selected to match the stone used in the back garden, which Charlotte also designed.

Passageways & steps

If ever there was a candidate for transformation, passageways, stairwells and steps must top the list. These often ignored places can all be beautiful.

Function first

Functionality is paramount, and movement through these areas should never be impeded. Narrow passageways may be able to accommodate only a built-in storage bench or a couple of wall-mounted baskets (which helpfully also 'ceiling' the void). Large steps can house a few pots, but thin stairwells will have room for only an annual climber like morning glory (*Ipomoea*), or runner beans, planted at the bottom and trained through the balusters, to leave the treads clear.

Boundary blues

A particularly dominant feature in courtyards, basements and passageways are their boundaries. Don't ignore them; they need to be tackled first.

Dilapidated fencing needs replacing. Hardwoods last longer and weather beautifully. Softwoods are cheaper,

Above: Given a wide stairwell it's possible to place plants on the treads. Safety is very important, so plants should never make access difficult.

Opposite: Tall buildings will dwarf a passageway and make it feel like the bottom of a deep gorge. Overhead beams, wall baskets or the arching canopy of bamboos or trees like these Japanese maples (*Acer palmatum*) will visually shrink the space into a smaller human scale.

Below: Wooden strip cladding creates a crisp modern look, and can mask ugly boundaries. For either hardwood or softwood, treat with ultraviolet-resistant preservative/oil to keep it looking like new.

but those orange panels are too lurid – use dark green or brown, ecofriendly preservative so they blend into any planting. Black or dark grey fencing is used by some designers, but not for large areas – it's too depressing.

PRACTICAL MATTERS

Storage: Bins are necessary, though an eyesore. Build a bin store to hide them.

Pipes: Ugly water and soil pipes can spoil a design. A coat of paint goes a long way. Or encourage non-invasive, lightweight climbers such as *Rhodochiton atrosanguineus* to cover them.

Cleaning: In shade, dark surface materials are preferable – algae on them isn't so obvious. Clean surfaces regularly, particularly decking.

Security: Side passageways are obvious points of attack for burglars. Grow spiky firethorn (*Pyracantha*) or climbing roses (*Rosa*) through thin trellis atop gates and boundaries, to make climbing over them more difficult.

Above, left: Colourful containers slung from the balustrades help to keep this narrow attractive stairwell as open as possible.

Above, right: With relatively little expense, narrow passageways can be transformed into fantastic gardens in their own right, but a wider space is necessary if you wish to include trees that grow to this size. Choose your plants carefully.

Replacing a structurally sound wall is expensive. Instead mask it with woven bamboo or willow screens secured to timber battens fixed to the wall behind. Concrete render, which can be coloured with certain sands, cements and dyes, is a possible option too. However, where space is tight, texture and pattern are important. Include sections of trellis, cedar strips (with a 2–3mm/$^1/_{12}$–$^1/_8$in shadow gap between each one) or even metal sheets, to add interest. Real stone panels commonly used in interior design can also work well – just make sure they're suitable for outdoor use.

Fast-growing but tidy climbers are the cheapest way to cover an ugly boundary and can help make the garden feel bigger by blending it into the surroundings. Boston ivy (*Parthenocissus tricuspidata*) and English ivy (*Hedera helix*) are perfect, but they will take a few years to get up to speed, even if you buy big specimens. They'll also need planting in the ground, as vigorous climbers in containers grow poorly. Alternatively how about a 'living' wall using ferns and ground cover (see p144)?

On the level

Surface materials should echo those in the main garden, to unite the two areas. To trick the eye into thinking a thin passageway is wider than it actually is, lay materials – paving or deck boards, for example – at an angle to adjacent boundaries. These will lead the eye across the space. Granite setts, clay pavers and oak sleepers laid in strips across the space have a similar effect.

Budget-friendly gravel is also an option. But think about how you use the space; gravel isn't suitable for wheeled rubbish bins, and it can't be swept easily either. Rather than remove it, cover ugly concrete with a thin layer of 8–15mm ($^{1}/_{3}$–$^{1}/_{2}$in) gravel, but ensure it doesn't block gully drains; a brick 'collar' around the top is usually necessary. Of course a sound concrete slab might allow you to lay thin textured tiles straight on top, instead (provided it doesn't compromise the damp-proof course of the house).

Tunnel vision

By their very nature, long passageways encourage tunnel vision. With all the emphasis on the end, a strong focal point is essential to 'reward' the eye. In a very small garden with a side passage, it's just a case of ensuring the garden's focal point is positioned with the passageway, as well as the lounge or kitchen, in mind.

Adding steps

A simple change of level to make a design more interesting is easy to introduce, but a longer flight of steps needs careful consideration. Be generous with the size; outdoor steps should be deeper and wider than those indoors. The riser (the vertical face) should ideally be 14–16cm (5$^{1}/_{2}$–6$^{1}/_{2}$in) high – and never higher than 20cm (8in). The tread should be 30–50cm (12–20in) deep.

Top: A landing on a series of steps allows for a place to rest and can indicate a change in direction. On long flights and for people with disabilities a landing for each 1.2m (4ft) flight of steps is desirable.

Above: Together with the light-coloured paving, these polished steel planters punch light into what might otherwise be a dark and gloomy side passage.

CASE STUDY

The perfect passage

Lynne Marcus designed this shady passageway, which is wrapped around two sides of a new modern townhouse. Her design shows that, with creativity, every centimetre of outdoor space can be made into a beautiful garden.

Just because the space might be small and shady (side passageways often are) doesn't mean it's suitable for only tiny plants. Think big. Perhaps, think jungle – just as Lynne has done here. She has given strong emphasis to form and texture. The tree ferns (*Dicksonia*), maples (*Acer*) and underplanting revel in the shade and give this corner a special atmosphere.

Eventually the informal 'jungle' gives way to more formal woodland, backed with tall golden bamboo (*Phyllostachys aurea*) to offer privacy from the neighbours, but they don't block out light. To mark the change and reference the clean modern architecture, a linear boardwalk runs though the space to a sculpture at the end. Chosen to pique interest but not to create a 'full

stop', the sculpture draws the eye through to the main garden, glimpses of which can also be seen through the glass of the family room overlooking the area.

To connect each space, Lynne used planting with similar colours, forms and textures. This can be done by selecting some of the same plants. But if one area is shady and the other is in sun this can be tricky. Fortunately many plants tolerate both sun and semishade: ideal are *Libertia grandiflora*, box (*Buxus*), plaintain lily (*Hosta*), bloody cranesbill (*Geranium sanguineum*), *Astelia chathamica*, purple coral flower (*Heuchera*), *Hakonechloa macra* 'Aureola', *Viburnum davidii* and the designer favourite, *Pittosporum tobira* 'Nanum'. There are hundreds of different ferns too.

Left: Tree ferns and maples 'ceiling' the space and enhance the delightful ambience.

Below: Ground cover like *Lamium maculatum* 'White Nancy', *Heuchera micrantha* var. *diversifolia* 'Palace Purple', shield fern (*Polystichum*) and lady's mantle (*Alchemilla mollis*) love semishade.

WHY THIS PASSAGEWAY WORKS

· Careful appreciation of the semishady conditions have determined the selection
  of plants, and inspired the aesthetic
· Simple palette of budget-friendly materials makes the whole space feel bigger
· Charming tapestry of easy-care, maintenance-free planting with a strong
  emphasis on form and texture

Above: The boardwalk distinguishes this part
of the passageway from the space before it, but
with their similar planting both areas share an
all-important connection.

Basements

At first, basements might seem like dark and dirty spaces fit only for rubbish bins or recycling boxes. In fact they're prime real estate bursting with potential.

The golden rule is big is best, even if you have only a small lightwell with little room for a potted plant, let alone a lounger. Limit choice to one key feature or a few specimen plants in attractive containers. With the often damp, warm, protected microclimate in mind, you could fill the space with fountain bamboo (*Fargesia nitida*), tree ferns (*Cyathea*), papyrus

(*Cyperus papyrus*), *Ligularia*, *Aruncus* and *Rodgersia podophylla* if they won't block too much light – the lush 'jungle' look works really well here. Grow plants in containers if the basement is covered in concrete or the soil's too dry to plant directly into it.

A lack of light

Not all basements (and side passageways too, for that matter) are dark and dingy, but lack of light is a common problem. You can lighten the mood with pale sandstone or travertine flooring, although you should attend to walls first as they dominate in basements. Relaying a new floor will cost a lot more too.

Painting walls a lighter colour creates a more airy atmosphere, but avoid bright white as it dirties easily. Instead go for a chalkier white; or choose a paler tint of a colour used in the home, to forge those all-important links. Avoid painting brick walls in good condition; paint is impossible to get rid of without sandblasting, which is a costly and very messy process. Scrubbing a dirty wall with hot soapy water is usually enough to make the whole space feel brighter.

Any reflective surface will add a little light: shiny pots and furniture, still pools – even glossy-leaved plants like Japanese aralia (*Fatsia japonica*). Mirrors can seemingly double the size of any space, but big is always best – tiny mirrors look odd. However, the success of a mirror is all in the illusion; simply reflecting the bins or your interior is pointless, so subtly angle each mirror to reflect planting instead. Try to hide the edges with climbers or wall claddings.

Glass mirrors aren't suitable for this; instead use acrylic, which is safer and easier to mount. Mirrored stainless steel is equally effective but costs a lot. Mirrors in gardens are somewhat controversial as birds crash into them, or fight their reflections. In basements or narrow alleyways, it's unlikely they'll cause problems.

Climbers can be used to clad basement walls, but try to leave gaps, or you'll create a gloomy atmosphere.

Privacy

Creating some privacy from above is usually necessary. Permanent shade-sails and overhead beams covered in climbers work well in courtyard gardens or areas linked to ground-floor flats. However in a basement these can make the space feel more claustrophobic, and they also cut out invaluable light. Fixed retractable awnings are a possible solution, as are canvas umbrellas. They're quick to erect and easy to handle, with a place for winter storage being the only issue with them.

A small tree in a container can offer overhead privacy. Deciduous birch (*Betula*), *Stewartia pseudocamellia* and Japanese maple (*Acer palmatum*) aren't overly dense, and cast less shade than an evergreen species.

Plants

Many beginner-gardeners view shade as a troublesome characteristic, but hundreds of fantastic plants thrive where light is limited. Admittedly you'll struggle to find lots of hot reds and oranges. But calming blue, soft pink and white flowers in particular are everywhere. Green, in all its shades and tints, is more important than ever. Texture and form from ferns, plantain lily (*Hosta*), box (*Buxus*), periwinkle (*Vinca*) and stinking iris (*Iris foetidissima*) play a big part too.

Silver foliage – a favourite for contrast – is also hard to come by, this being a natural adaptation to reflect strong sun. For this reason *Lamium maculatum* 'Beacon Silver', *Astelia chathamica* 'Silver Spear', *Brunnera macrophylla* 'Jack Frost', *Dicentra formosa* 'Langtrees' and *Plectranthus argentatus* are invaluable as they thrive in all but the deepest shade.

PRACTICAL MATTERS

Access: Consider access to basements for maintenance. If this is a struggle then stick to tidy, low-maintenance evergreens like box, bamboo and palms that need little care and attention.

Drainage: Surfaces should always drain to a storm-water drain. In areas with a high water table, and therefore permanently wet soil, choose moisture-loving baneberry (*Actaea*), arum lily (*Zantedeschia*), cyperus, astilbe and Himalayan honeysuckle (*Leycesteria formosa*) or grow plants in raised beds (which could double up as seats) or in containers.

Surface: Removing existing concrete is costly and tricky. However, if kept, it could be the perfect sub-base for thinner slabs or tiles (if adding them won't compromise the damp-proof course of the house).

Top: A lightwell might not be large enough to be a truly practical space but it should still be 'greened' so that the view from inside is attractive.

Above: Light-coloured paving, paint and mirrors (cleverly made to look like windows) reflect light into the small basement. Together they help make it feel more spacious than it actually is.

Left: In shady basements opt for eye-catching forms and textures – such as those of ferns, tree ferns (*Dicksonia*), greater woodrush (*Luzula sylvatica*) and astelia – as flowering perennials and shrubs are unlikely to flourish.

CASE STUDY

Light down below

This previously gloomy basement has seen a masterful transformation by designer George Carter. Based on a strong layout and careful attention to detail, it's designed to work from all angles, including looking down on the basement from above.

To bring light and life into the space George employed all manner of classic tricks. The black pool in the middle catches the sun and reflects passing clouds, forging a relationship with the sky. Plants such as arum lily (*Zantedeschia*), *Pittosporum tobira* 'Nanum' and *Cyrtomium fortunei* were chosen for their glossy green foliage. Low-voltage uplighters shoot fans of light skyward at night (these also cast moody shadows through foliage).

Moving water makes a great focal point and gives some distraction from street sounds. For a water feature, George adapted a period metal fireplace loved by his client. With the spout and a waterproof uplighter underneath to cast flickering, flame-like effects, it's now

a quirky feature, day and night. Importantly it works visually even when the water isn't on – something to consider when choosing a water feature for any small garden.

The steps above provide an element of overhead privacy, but George has also included clipped hornbeam (*Carpinus*) 'lollipops'. These add a big splash of green and 'ceiling' the garden without blocking out light. Elsewhere every wall has been utilised for planting, but not so much that it takes over. Honeysuckle (*Lonicera*), clematis and star jasmine (*Trachelospermum jasminoides*) climb bespoke trellis. Shallow shelves high up are positioned to house sun-loving herbs and succulents but aren't deep enough to shade the space below.

Left: A fireplace focal point 'anchors' the eye in the space and helps stop it being overwhelmed by the buildings all around.

Below: Galvanised steel panels fitted behind the bespoke trellis reflect light.

WHY THIS BASEMENT GARDEN WORKS

· Simple layout, very economical with space
· Light and airy atmosphere created through careful detailed design
· Slip-resistant surface materials in keeping with the period architecture
· Shade-tolerant planting with year-round interest doesn't dominate or overwhelm the space

Above: For safety, flooring in basements should have a slip-resistant finish. Here, old stable bricks were chosen, which also beautifully complement the period architecture of the building and the wrought-iron steps.

Roof terraces & balconies

Balcony and roof-terrace design has much in common with interior design, being more about adding accessories to a space than about wholesale structural change. Changes to, or fixings into, the fabric of the building aren't usually an option, because of building regulations or prohibitive expense.

Whatever you do, keep it simple. Balconies in particular are rarely big enough to accommodate more than a bistro table and chairs, a lounger or sometimes only a few pots. Exercise restraint, or you'll make your interior feel cramped and claustrophobic.

For these 'outdoor rooms', take a lead from the interior when choosing materials – even plants. Those that complement patterns or colours from indoors help create a seamless transition between inside and out.

Views

Gardens up high are essentially giant windows onto the world. Make the most of this when choosing or positioning plants and features: for example, frame the best views with columnar junipers (*Juniperus*); or pick a sculpture that has some similarity to a key building on the horizon.

Overexposure

Wind exposure is a common problem on balconies and roof terraces. Solid windbreaks are a poor choice, because they block the view, and strong gusts also slam against them and rush over the top with considerable force. Instead choose perforated sailcloth, trelliswork or spaced cedar battens, which all filter the wind as well as maximise light levels.

Where there's room, some protection is afforded in the lee of wind-tolerant shrubs such as phormium, pittosporum and daisy bush (*Olearia*). In very gusty

Right: A small balcony should be kept clutter-free, so keep the furnishings and plantings simple. Consider the home when it comes to design details, and embrace the view!

Above: An exposed urban roof terrace shares a similarity to a seaside cliff top; that's certainly been the inspiration here, literally!

Left: With protection it's possible to grow a wide range of plants like these, but in an exposed spot your first choice of plants should be those with silvery, thick-waxy, hairy or needle-like leaves, and mounding forms that have naturally adapted to such conditions.

exposed spots, avoid plants with a big 'sail' area; these dry out quickly and never establish well, being constantly rocked by the wind in their pots.

For shelter from hot sun, once again wind-porous materials are best. Fixed shade-sails are popular, but a sturdy parasol or even a temporary, Bedouin-style sheet slung between strong supports gives more flexible use.

Plants

Plants should be wind- and drought-tolerant and also cope with sun or shade, depending on their position. A few key specimens are sometimes all that's needed. Whatever you choose they should look good for as long a time as possible, as there probably won't be room or sufficient support on the roof for extensive collections.

Clifftop maritime and seaside plants are suitable for exposed roof terraces or balconies. Alpines, dwarf pines (*Pinus*), mounding hebes and Mediterranean herbs like thyme (*Thymus*) and lavender (*Lavandula*) are ideal. Avoid bamboos and jungly bananas (*Musa*) unless the balcony is well protected – these dry out fast.

PRACTICAL MATTERS

Weight: For the load-bearing capacity of balconies and purpose-built roof terraces, check the title deeds of your home. With older properties, seek the services of a structural engineer, who will calculate how much weight the roof can cope with and where it should be distributed. (A new roof terrace will inevitably need planning permission.)

If weight is an issue, fibreglass pots weigh less than stone or terracotta ones. For drainage use polystyrene chunks rather than gravel or terracotta crocks (see p190). Coir or bark-based potting composts are lighter than soil-based ones. Fixing pots to surrounding walls will help, in that the walls, not the roof, will be taking the weight. If you cannot secure the pots to the walls, at the very least place the pots close to the walls, again so they take more of the weight, and don't have too many.

Safety: Anything hanging over an edge is potentially a hazard unless it's firmly secured. Handrails should be a minimum height (in the UK it's 1.1m/3½ft high). Factor this in carefully if raising the floor height with decking or paving.

Access: Take into account the width of stairwells and doorways for delivery of plants and materials.

Irrigation: A watering system with timer is useful, but not all spaces have an outside tap. Restrict plantings to the number you can cope with by hand watering.

Rules & regulations: Most flats and apartments are subject to strict rules and covenants for any changes other than plants in pots. Structures such as pergolas and even painting railings or a handrail usually need permission from the appropriate authority.

Up on the roof

A private retreat away from the busy city streets has been radically improved by designer Sara-Jane Rothwell. This urban rooftop garden is the perfect place for sky-high, alfresco entertaining.

No one can argue that roof terraces and balconies suffer from a 'lack of landscape'; they're positively dominated by it. To reflect this, Sara-Jane has here opted for a clean layout and a modern use of materials.

Weathered stock bricks and honey-coloured decking are a classic combination, and together with other materials echo the lines and colours in surrounding buildings. In turn this helps to blend the design subtly into the skyline.

Decking is the perfect choice for roof terraces and balconies, because it's warm for bare feet and very easy

to work with. Joists can be fixed to surrounding walls to keep the weight off the roof itself, and storm water can still run underneath to the existing drain system. Sara-Jane chose western red cedar here, but hardwoods like ipe or yellow balau (bought from a sustainable source – look for an FSC or PEFC label) are also good choices. Cleverly the designer has used the same material to make a long, built-in bench – a great space saver, with real sculptural quality.

This garden is about much more than the city beyond it, though. As Sara-Jane remarks, 'It was just crying

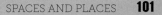

Above: This rooftop was functional, yet dirty and dingy, before its transformation. But look at that view!

Right: The chosen plants both soften and complement the strong geometry of the surroundings.

Below: Borrowing scenery is the easiest way to make a space feel bigger, and what better focal point than a church steeple.

Above: A simple, elegant yet abundant design blends seamlessly into its surroundings, through clever planting and detailed design.

out for plants!' The boundaries are hidden with terraced galvanised planters that help elevate the plants and surround the terrace with colour. To unify the space, swathes of wildlife-friendly *Sedum* 'Matrona', feather grass (*Stipa tenuissima*), *Penstemon* 'Andenken an Friedrich Hahn', toadflax (*Linaria purpurea*), *Achillea millefolium* 'Cerise Queen' and *Gaura lindheimeri* are repeated throughout in a modern prairie-style meadow planting, which softens and contrasts with the strong geometry.

WHY THIS ROOFTOP GARDEN WORKS

- Functional and flexible space in which to relax, eat and entertain
- Strong appreciation of location and surrounding architecture
- Modern but limited materials palette
- Bold simple layout
- Easy-care, wildlife-friendly planting tolerant of drought and exposure

PLANTING THE URBAN GARDEN

Plants are the heart and soul of an urban garden. They introduce colour and sweet scent into our lives, tasty produce to our tables, and bring us in closer contact with the natural world – something we often forget when caught up in the hustle and bustle of city life.

Plants are vital guardians for urban wildlife; trees, in particular, shelter and offer food to many different birds, mammals, insects and invertebrates that often support us in our gardening endeavours. With their pollinating or pest-feeding activities, they help to encourage bigger and better blooms or fatter fruit and veg.

Designing with plants is particularly exciting, as there are so many to choose from, in every single colour, size and shape, and for every environment imaginable.

In addition, no other art form allows you to work with such spectacular seasonal change. From the brilliant yellows of spring to the fiery oranges of autumn, changes are always afoot as the gardening year passes. With careful planning, there can be something new to look at every couple of weeks.

I will admit that beginner gardeners find plants somewhat daunting, but, believe me, you're not born with green fingers. They grow on you, and it doesn't take long. There's inspiration aplenty, from books to public gardens to famous flower shows, and soon you will learn to create exciting combinations to stimulate the senses. This chapter will help you design with plants, but do learn to love their unpredictability; some of the most amazing combinations happen by accident!

Right plant, right place

With so many plants available, how do you choose? First it's important to pick plants to match your particular garden, following the old adage of right plant, right place. Sun-loving plants require sun, shade-lovers need shade, and pond plants must have lots of water, whereas cacti require virtually none. Forcing plants to grow where they're not happy will result in stressed plants that are susceptible to pests and diseases, requiring lots of extra tender loving care.

Some characteristics can be controlled by design – hedges positioned to filter strong winds, or garden lime used to amend soil acidity, for example – but sometimes these solutions aren't sustainable. I find it's usually best to work with what you've got.

Opposite: For a lot of people, myself included, plants bring so much more beauty to a garden than extensive hard landscaping; many can perform invaluable design roles too.

Right: On hot windy roof terraces, it's imperative to pick plants such as purple top (*Verbena bonariensis*), blue fescue (*Festuca*), African blue lily (*Agapanthus*), southernwood (*Artemisia abrotanum*), agave and dwarf fan palm (*Chamaerops humilis*), which can naturally adapt to such harsh conditions.

Clues from nature

The easiest way to get plants right is to choose those whose natural habitat is similar to that of your garden. For exposed roof terraces, alpines and seaside plants like valerian (*Centranthus*) and thrift (*Armeria*) are ideal. For damp basements, go for moist, shade-loving woodland ferns and plantain lilies (*Hosta*). Choosing plants compatible with their environment means they're also more likely to combine visually, as each one will share similar features (such as leaf size, shape or colour) having probably grown together in the wild.

Looking to nature for help doesn't mean you need expertise in ecology. Some garden-makers look to where plants grow naturally in the wild for design inspiration and to help them deal with problem areas in the garden. Such an approach is exemplified by gardener Beth Chatto and designers Dan Pearson, Wolfgang Oehme, James van Sweden and Piet Oudolf.

Above: Plants can evoke a particular place through association. Here shadbush (*Amelanchier*) trees underplanted with ferns give this city front garden a real edge-of-woodland feel.

Below: Ferns, ivy (*Hedera*), coral flower (*Heuchera*) and elephant's ears (*Bergenia*) are all thriving on a living wall in this shady side passageway – similar conditions to where you'd find them growing happily in the wild.

WHAT YOU NEED TO KNOW

As well as climate (see p105) and soil, it's also important to understand plant behaviour. This affects how and where plants work best.

LIFECYCLES

Annuals & biennials

Annuals live for a year; biennials (*eg* foxgloves/ *Digitalis* and forget-me-nots/*Myosotis*) for two. Half-hardy bedding annuals (*eg* snapdragons/ *Antirrhinum* and busy lizzies/*Impatiens*) won't tolerate frost; hardy annuals and biennials will. All flower fast. Sow half-hardy annuals in trays under cover, then plant out once all danger of frost has passed; sow hardy annuals *in situ*. Usefully, biennials and some hardy annuals readily self-seed.

Perennials

Quick-growing plants including catmint (*Nepeta*) and stonecrop (*Sedum*) bring long-lasting interest but don't develop a woody structure. Ferns, ornamental grasses, many alpines and most pond plants also fall into this group. Some perennials are evergreen, but the majority are herbaceous, dying back underground over winter to re-emerge in spring. Many form clumps or dense mats; others spread by creeping runners or rhizomes.

Bulbs, corms & tubers

Bulbs (*eg* daffodils/*Narcissus*), corms (*eg* crocus) and tubers (*eg* winter aconite/*Eranthis hyemalis*) are also herbaceous but have food storage organs that enable them to remain dormant for long periods, before bursting into growth when conditions are perfect, usually early in the year.

Trees & shrubs

Permanent woody structures with usually one stem, if a tree; shrubs have many stems. Conifers and evergreen trees and shrubs (and climbers) retain their leaves over winter; deciduous ones don't.

Climbers

Most (*eg* wisteria) are woody, but fast-growers (*eg* sweet peas/*Lathyrus odoratus*) are annuals. Some need sturdy support; others (*eg* ivy/*Hedera*) climb unaided. A few shrubs also enjoy the support and warmth of a wall.

Right: Bulbs such as ornamental onions (*Allium*) are brilliant in small urban gardens. When planted to grow through frothy perennials (which also help hide their straggly stems) it's possible to get bursts of colour at different times from the same space.

Size & vigour

Huge plants in urban gardens don't work, as they need constant pruning and quickly outgrow their surroundings. But vigour is just as important. Unless they're used in isolation, invasive spreaders are poor choices; they'll quickly take over. But sometimes normally well-behaved plants – especially marginal plants and perennials from warmer climates – also assume a thuggish persona, especially if crammed together in thin borders. Even when faced with limited space, always site plants with both their vigour and size at maturity in mind, and be prepared to divide perennials and prune shrubs more than usual.

With trees it's particularly important to select ones of appropriate size and vigour for your site. Consider 'slow growers' carefully too – slow growing does not always mean small when mature.

How much maintenance?

Maintenance is a key factor when identifying plants to include in your garden. Just how much time do you have? High-maintenance gardens feature a lawn, fruit and vegetables, collections of tiny containers, lots of annuals, biennials, topiary, bush roses and tall perennials, which need staking. Easy-care, low-maintenance schemes use lots of shrubs, conifers, ornamental grasses, shrub roses, sturdy clump-forming perennials and non-invasive groundcover plants. And remember, there is no such thing as a 'no-maintenance' garden.

Existing planting

Mature trees and larger shrubs offer a wealth of benefits such as privacy and habitats for urban wildlife. Think carefully before you remove them. A tree might

Right: Apart from a little weeding and the thinning of oxygenators in the pool, this dramatic jungle grove full of giant moso bamboo (*Phyllostachys edulis*), ferns and palms needs very little maintenance.

Below: Extensive, perennial-heavy schemes, here including foxgloves (*Digitalis*), white dusky cranesbill (*Geranium phaeum* 'Album') and alpine columbine (*Aquilegia alpina*), require quite a bit of care to work well.

shade the lawn, but is this bad enough to warrant its removal? It might be doing the perfect job of screening an eyesore that you won't notice until you've chopped the tree down. It might well be better to see if a tree surgeon can work wonders with some judicious pruning. Sometimes however you do have to be ruthless, but don't axe mature plants without thought; you might really miss them when they're gone.

Small trees and shrubs situated in the wrong place (or planting combinations that didn't work, for that matter) can all be rehomed (see p110). A key to success is to minimise damage to the root system. Small plants are fine to move yourself. But you will need assistance for trees with a trunk diameter larger than 12–14cm (5–6in) and for shrubs higher than head height, because at these sizes they'll be awkward to shift.

Moving plants in the wrong place

In cool-temperate climates, deciduous shrubs, roses and trees are best moved between late autumn and early spring; evergreens and conifers between early and mid-autumn or in early or mid-spring.

Small roses and deciduous hedging (less than 50cm/20in high) can be lifted bare root (free from soil). However, to transplant larger deciduous trees and shrubs and all evergreen ones successfully, you'll need to include a ball of soil with as many roots as is practically possible, particularly the young fibrous or 'feeder' roots.

1 Choose a dry day when the ground's not frozen or waterlogged. Loosely gather and tie up shoots and branches, then scrape away any mulch so that you can easily get to the roots.

2 As a guide: cut at least 30cm (12in) away for shrubs 1.2–1.5m (4–5ft) high and for three- to four-year-old trees; for plants like magnolia and daphne that hate having their roots disturbed, go wider still; for perennials and new shrubs, 15–20cm (6–8in) away is fine. Cut around the plant in a circle, keeping the spade upright while wiggling it from side to side in a scissor-like motion; don't start to lever out the plant.

3 Once you've sliced around the whole plant, sink the spade under the rootball as deeply as possible in different spots until any roots underneath have been broken or cut loose. Use loppers or a saw for thick roots. With very large plants, dig a narrow deep trench around the outside, then undercut from one side to the other from the trench with a spade; this helps to minimise unnecessary damage.

6 Replant to the same depth as before in the new garden position. If you don't want to replant straight away, keep the rootball covered with sacking or tarpaulin so it doesn't dry out. After planting, water well and mulch with a layer of compost 10cm (4in) thick. Trees above 1.5m (5ft) will need staking (for support).

4 Small plants will lift out easily. For larger ones the rootball will need to be carefully supported. Enlist a helper, each person sliding a spade underneath to take the weight, before lifting the rootball onto a tarpaulin. Never lift the plant by the stem alone. For larger plants use the tarpaulin as a sling. Slide it underneath the rootball, then collect the corners and lift it together with the plant out of the hole. Soil type affects how the rootball holds together. Sticky clay soils make for easy moving, but sandy soils crumble quickly and need handling with extra care.

5 After lifting, lightly trim back damaged roots with secateurs, leaving a clean cut.

Above: When given water in dry spells for the first year or so and a sprinkling of general fertiliser such as blood, fish and bone each spring for 2–3 years, transplants should re-establish well.

Urban planting design principles

Simplicity

Where every centimetre is precious, space for plants will always compete with space for living. A restrained palette of plants always works best, whether you decide to create a lush urban oasis or pare back plantings to sculptural specimens. Sadly there's never room for all your favourites, trust me!

Style & theme

Many plants come packed with personality and sometimes just one is enough to swing a scheme in a particular direction. Clipped topiary evokes a classic formal style, whereas blousy summer clematis suggests relaxed, informal romance. Some plants are synonymous with certain themes; bamboos and Japanese maples (*Acer palmatum*) suggest an Oriental garden whereas exotic bananas (*Musa*) and ginger lily (*Hedychium*) point to a tropical jungle. To bring unity to the whole design always let your chosen style or theme dictate the plants you use.

In recent years naturalistic styles have been particularly popular, but they rarely work in small gardens. You need space to appreciate them, and they're reliant on annuals or mid- to late-season perennials for interest, meaning lots of gaps over winter and spring.

That's not to say you should ignore them completely. Tiny urban gardens might work well with architectural evergreens, but in larger suburban ones there's no reason why you can't turn part of the lawn into a mini-meadow, particularly if it backs onto woodland or parkland. This can be a great way to encourage beneficial wildlife and cut down on maintenance.

Harmony, repetition & rhythm

Repetition is what divides a 'designed' planting scheme from one that's simply 'evolved'. It brings a sense of 'oneness' to a scheme and helps to impose a little order – no bad thing if there's a lot competing for your attention in the garden.

Above: The purple cranesbill (*Geranium*) and silvery grey lavender (*Lavandula*) are vital in this scheme, being the repetitive element that helps to tie the rest of the planting together.

Repetition also brings rhythm to your planting, as it does in music, which helps to make sense of the composition. Natural flowing rhythms come from plantings arranged in graceful drifts. A regular rhythm occurs when one plant or similar groups of plants are spaced equidistantly or the groups themselves are the same in size or length. Progressive rhythms follow a sequence of steps in height or colour – red evolving into orange, then into yellow, for example. Use this to point the way from one space to another perhaps.

Layers of interest

Plants are always arranged in layers, with height in mind. In small gardens this makes good use of space, but each plant also becomes the foil for others around it. Importantly taller plants are less likely to cast shade on smaller plants too. Because of their size, trees, large shrubs and climbers form the background layer; smaller shrubs, roses and taller perennials are in the middle; while shorter perennials and most bulbs occupy the ground layer down in front of the bed or border.

Above: Repetition, particularly in the foreground or 'carpet' layer like this, allows the viewer to make seemingly unconscious, satisfying connections between similar forms and colours.

Below: In this simple but effective woodland planting design, flowering dogwood trees (*Cornus*), ferns and big blue lilyturf (*Liriope muscari*), edging the path, are arranged in layers with height in mind.

Colour

Above: This red 'ribbon' of *Papaver commutatum* 'Ladybird' (alongside mauve *Geranium pyrenaicum* 'Bill Wallis') really stands out because of the green around it – green being its complementary colour.

Colour is one of the most powerful design tools available. It can create an atmosphere, influence emotions and even make your garden feel bigger.

Colour & atmosphere

For calm and tranquillity use soft cool colours like pale yellow, light blue and pale pink. Warm nurturing neutrals have a similar effect but include plants with lots of different texture for added interest. Nurturing green is particularly useful for its ability to calm and revitalise the spirits.

Bright hot colours are lively and exciting. If you crave sensory stimulation go for orange, red and yellow.

Although technically not true colours, silver and white help soothe 'loud' combinations. Usefully they bring out the best of recessive colours like blue. Both silver and white also stand out on overcast days.

Our perception of colour

Colour can affect our perception of size. Dominant colours like orange arrest the eye, so use these close to the house, not on the back boundary. At the back, introduce cooler colours, which recede into the distance, giving the illusion of depth.

A background has a strong influence on the effect of colours in front of it: for example, purple against a dark green backdrop will blend in, whereas purple against apple green will stand out. Consider this carefully, particularly if painting 'feature' walls and then planting in front of them.

Light has an impact on colour too. In sun, colours appear bolder and brighter. In shade, they're softer and flatter. This explains why vivid Mediterranean blues don't work well in cool-temperature areas, where the light is greyer, so earthier tones look best.

Right, top: This harmonious green scheme with silver *Verbascum bombyciferum* 'Polarsommer' and white *Salvia* x *sylvestris* 'Schneehügel' uses an eye-catching mix of contrasting plant form and texture.

Right, centre: Orange-brown *Achillea* 'Walther Funcke' and blue globe onion (*Allium caeruleum*), surrounded by pheasant's tail grass (*Anemanthele lessoniana*), form a lovely complementary combination.

Right, bottom: A harmonious mauve, purple and blue colour scheme featuring lavender (*Lavandula*), cottage pinks (*Dianthus*) and trailing bellflower (*Campanula poscharskyana*) is here backed by star jasmine (*Trachelospermum jasminoides*).

THE COLOUR WHEEL

As used by artists and designers, the colour wheel is an invaluable starting point when considering how to combine colour effectively.

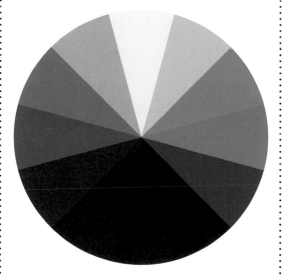

Harmonious planting schemes pick colours adjacent to each other: *eg* blue, purple and mauve; or red, yellow and orange. It's the easiest way to achieve a coherent look.

Complementary combinations use colours that are opposite each other on the colour wheel: *eg* canary yellow and violet. These associations are intense and can overpower, especially in a small garden, so site them carefully. For 'calmer' contrasts choose pastels and paler tints: *eg* primrose yellow with chalky mauve.

Monochromatic plantings are made from various shades and tints of one colour. They are useful as calm patches to link other combinations, but perhaps boring on a grand scale.

Polychromatic (& triadic) combinations of violets, reds, blues, yellows and oranges are incredibly exciting but need careful thought in their use. This look works well when mixing wilder perennials with oatmeal-coloured grasses, but not when planting bold blocks of summer bedding.

Form & texture

A plant's form – simplistically, its shape in three dimensions – is its most striking characteristic, and the one that designers typically work with first. All plant forms have some sculptural qualities but some are stronger than others. Columnar, spiky or weeping plants make great focal points either by themselves (in a container perhaps) or as a punctuation point among others – a pencil juniper (*Juniperus*) to lift the eye skyward, for example. Softer, rounded and horizontal forms are just as important. These are relaxing to look at and provide contrast to bold forms.

A plant's outline isn't the only thing to consider. Flowers and seedheads are full of form too: for example, foxtail lily (*Eremurus*) has erect spires, while those of yarrow (*Achillea filipendulina*) are broad and flat. You might decide to juxtapose different forms together for contrast, or to blend similar ones for a more harmonious look.

The golden rule is don't mix lots of strong forms, as too much contrast will be uncomfortable to look at. Instead, stick to two or three, perhaps adding another as a focal point to contrast with plants around it.

A plant's texture is the surface appearance of its leaves, bark, flowers, seedheads and fruit. It can only really be appreciated up close. Texture abounds: glossy or matt finishes are affected by light; furry or downy textures just have to be stroked! In monochromatic plantings, foliage-heavy jungles or tiny gardens with just a few evergreens, include lots of contrasting textures to spice things up a bit. Consider the appearance of hardscape materials too.

Left: Flowers and seedheads come packed with form. With late flowerers such as stonecrop (*Sedum*) (**top**), artichoke (*Cynara scolymus*) (**centre**) and Turkish sage (*Phlomis russeliana*) (**bottom**) the seedheads will stand tall well into winter, for as long as the weather stays dry.

Scent

Above: In windy locations such as balconies and rooftops, low-growing plants like herbs with scented leaves are a better option than plants with floral scents, which will be whipped away by the wind before you have time to enjoy them.

Scent brings a delicious dimension to a planting scheme and can be used to intensify atmosphere in sun or shade year-round. If possible pick plants that punch out their perfume at different times. Some even save their scent for the evening, so try these if you want to relax outside or entertain after work – try night-scented stocks (*Matthiola longipetala* subsp. *bicornis*), moonflower (*Ipomoea alba*) and Madonna lilies (*Lilium candidum*).

I split scent into three groups, which helps organise where particular plants work best. These are: free scents; up-close scents; and touchy-feely scents.

Free scents are to be found in plants such as regal lily (*Lilium regale*), common jasmine (*Jasminum officinale*)

and honeysuckle (*Lonicera periclymenum* 'Graham Thomas'), which are liberal with a potent perfume, sometimes generous to a fault. They are ideal for masking seasonal city smells.

Up-close or personal scents are more subtle. Lilac (*Syringa*), viburnum and many roses (*Rosa*) are in this group. Shelter them close to the house or patio, so you don't have to travel far to appreciate them. Delicate scents like that of lily of the valley (*Convallaria*) need planting en masse to have any effect.

Touchy-feely scents come from leaves of plants like lavender (*Lavandula*) and sage (*Salvia*). Use them close to paths, patios or seating areas so they're in easy reach.

Above: In modern planting schemes full of herbaceous perennials, reliable grasses such as Mexican feather grass (*Stipa tenuissima*) have an important structural role and are commonly used in repetitive drifts.

Right: Black bamboo (*Phyllostachys nigra*) and clipped copper beech (*Fagus sylvatica* f. *purpurea*) screen this semisecret seating spot from the rest of the garden – much as a wall or fence would do.

The roles of plants

Good gardeners know that plants aren't just mere decorations; they also have other roles. To help organise what might go where, divide up your wish list of potential plants into two distinct groups: structural plants (those that hold the scheme together); and ornamental plants, which supply the majority of colour and interest. Some plants will fit into both categories but that's good, especially where space is limited.

The space makers

Structural plants – whether sizeable single specimens or collections of five to seven or more – form the framework or 'backbone' of a planting design. Most are modest in nature, yet have a presence that helps brings unity to the scheme. They also act as a foil to the more showy starlets and, if big enough, create pockets of space for us to appreciate smaller combinations that might otherwise get lost.

On a larger scale, structural plants can also make or define different spaces within the garden. These might be play spaces, entertainment areas or simply somewhere to empty the grass clippings.

Outside 'walls'

Hedges, shrubs, bamboos and long-lasting ornamental grasses form our 'walls' outside. In urban gardens reliability is important, so most structural plants are evergreen, although deciduous shrubs and hedges with strong form work well too. Design-wise these plants help give spaces their own identity, foster curiosity about what's around the corner, focus views from one

'room' to the next, and determine the direction when walking through the garden. If such plants are above head height they'll offer privacy and protection; if lower than that, they'll define one space from another without creating a hemmed-in feeling.

If you want high divisions where space is tight, formal hedges, 'pleached' trees (hedges on 'stilts' as I call them), clump-forming bamboos and lofty ornamental grasses like silver banner grass (*Miscanthus sacchariflorus*) are ideal as they're tall but thin and can be more easily squeezed in.

'Ceiling' a space

If hedges are the walls, then trees create a ceiling. Under the leaf canopy is a ready-made room for quiet contemplation, or a private dining area. Evergreens, especially those with a low canopy, make more intimate spaces. Less dense deciduous trees provide more airy spaces – perfect for alfresco dining. Try to strike a balance between the two, however, as tall evergreen trees or hedges might accidentally pitch parts of the garden into shade, especially in winter. Instead, a deciduous tree might be a better alternative.

Key or feature plants

These plants are structural plants too, but are usually the most distinctive of the bunch, so also help set the style or theme of the planting scheme. On their own, shrubs with strong form like phormium, palms and clipped topiary become useful focal points to draw the eye or highlight particular features. Perennials and ornamental grasses perform a similar role if used en masse, as well as helping to knit the planting together.

Infill plants

A big group, including smaller deciduous shrubs and roses (*Rosa*), ornamental grasses, perennials and annuals, fills in the space between structural evergreen and deciduous plants. Here you'll be able to play with colourful combinations and help reinforce a particular style or theme. I look at these plants as the stars of the show, but you can only appreciate their performance once the stage has been created by the structural plants.

Above: Bulbs such as ornamental onions (here *Allium* 'Mont Blanc') are perfect accents of form and colour. They contrast with the frothy infill around them. They would harmonise well with the box balls (**left**) too.

Left: With strong contrasting form, these box (*Buxus*) balls are big feature plants and help reinforce the design style. By repeating groups of them around the garden they have an important structural role.

Accents

These pick up on the character set by the key plants, but work to a smaller scale. Unlike key plants, accent ones don't perform well by themselves, so need planting in groups for impact. Drifts of striking bulbs or perennials such as ornamental onions (*Allium*), tulips (*Tulipa*) or gayfeather (*Liatris spicata*) are common, planted with cranesbill (*Geranium*) and lavender (*Lavandula*) for contrast. Accent plants are generally in the foreground, but in deeper borders they may also appear towards the back to draw the eye into the planting. If repeated or echoed through the scheme they help link it as well.

Ground cover

A disparate but important group of low-maintenance, spreading perennials, grasses, ferns, prostrate shrubs and conifers cover the soil surface, suppress weeds and also provide a rich tapestry of colour and texture, often all year round. Because of its size, most ground cover is positioned in the front of the border; however, it may be used further back, to give an illusion of depth.

In this role, repetition is very common, with the same or similar plants recurring throughout. For me, shorter ornamental grasses or perennials like catmint (*Nepeta*), masterwort (*Astrantia*) and elephant's ears (*Bergenia*) work really well; they're perfect with spring bulbs too.

Using their contrasting characteristics, mid-height plants should complement all those around them. That is, if surrounding plants have strong features, adjacent ones should possess more neutral qualities.

Towards the front of a bed or border, perennials are in the majority. However squat evergreen and deciduous shrubs (some called subshrubs) like lavender (*Lavandula*), sage (*Salvia*) and *Pittosporum tobira* 'Nanum' are widely used as a foil to the perennials.

Naturalising bulbs in grass, beds and borders and under trees

Bulbs are brilliant, bringing colour by the bucket load while taking up virtually no space at all. A favourite for pots, they also look good naturalised informally under trees, in mini-meadows or growing through frothy perennials such as cranesbill (*Geranium*).

Always let bulbs die back naturally, or at the very least leave them uncut for six weeks – the quality of next year's flowers depends on it. Consider this when positioning displays. Bulbs that have flowered look untidy for a little while. That's why, for bulbs, it's best to site them in parts of the lawn further away from the house or plant them among border perennials, which will hide the foliage as it dies down and yellows.

Almost all bulbs need fertile, free-draining soil to thrive, but a few such as fritillaries (*Fritillaria*), great quamash (*Camassia leichtlinii*) and dog's-tooth violet (*Erythronium dens-canis*) like slightly damp soil. Spring-flowering bulbs should be planted in autumn. Hardy, summer-flowering ones can be planted in autumn too, but leave tender bulbs such as Byzantine gladiolus (*Gladiolus communis* subsp. *byzantinus*) until spring.

BULBS (& CORMS, RHIZOMES) SUITABLE FOR NATURALISING

Sunny borders
- *Camassia leichtlinii* (great quamash)
- *Fritillaria meleagris* (snake's head fritillary)
- *Gladiolus communis* subsp. *byzantinus* (Byzantine gladiolus)
- *Leucojum aestivum* (summer snowflake)
- *Lilium martagon* (common turkscap lily)
- *Muscari latifolium* (grape hyacinth)
- *Narcissus obvallaris* (Tenby daffodil)
- *Narcissus poeticus* var. *recurvus* (old pheasant's eye)
- *Narcissus* 'Thalia'
- *Ornithogalum nutans* (Star-of-Bethlehem)

Semishady border/grass/woodlands/under trees
- *Anemone nemorosa* (wood anemone)
- *Chionodoxa luciliae* (glory of the snow)
- *Crocus chrysanthus* (early crocus)
- *Crocus tommasinianus* and cultivars (golden crocus)
- *Cyclamen coum* (eastern cyclamen)
- *Cyclamen hederifolium* (ivy-leaved cyclamen)
- *Eranthis hyemalis* (winter aconite)
- *Erythronium dens-canis* (dog's-tooth violet)
- *Galanthus nivalis* (common snowdrop)
- *Hyacinthoides non-scripta* (English bluebell)
- *Scilla siberica* (Siberian squill)

Opposite, top: Along with crocus, daffodils (*Narcissus*) are the easiest and least fussy bulbs to naturalise. They grow strongly on almost all but the wettest soils.

1 Find an area in a border or near the edge of the lawn where the grass could be allowed to grow long. To make planting easier in grass, cut the sward to the same height as normal. Then scatter bulbs randomly over the area to be planted. Drop handfuls from waist height – this helps give a natural look on the ground. If some fall close together, gently flick them apart. Informal, teardrop-shaped drifts are easier to mow in grass.

2 Plant each bulb where it falls, but aim for a minimum of at least twice the bulb's own width apart. Dig a hole three times the depth of the bulb. Use a traditional trowel or specialist bulb planter when planting bulbs in quantity.

3 Place the bulb in the hole with the pointed end or 'nose' facing upwards.

4 Then, using the soil you've dug out, cover the bulb with crumbled soil and firm *gently* with your hands. In a lawn, replace the tiny turf plug on the top. Water the area well if it's dry.

Mixed planting

In urban gardens, structural evergreens are the first choice; in fact, where space can't accommodate lots of plants, you may find only a few sculptural specimens. A line of black bamboo (*Phyllostachys nigra*) or topiary might have year-round presence, but does it provide year-round interest? With this in mind, where there's room, slip in annuals, bulbs, perennials, climbers and special deciduous shrubs, for seasonal colour. Usefully each group gives interest at different times during the year. Even in winter there can still be colourful stems, wildlife-friendly berries or quirky seedheads on show.

Making the most of the mix

Designing with plants for year-round interest can be tricky but here are some tips to help.

Containers are a great way to introduce temporary displays of vibrant colour using spring and summer bedding plants. Move them around and replace the plants when the whim takes you.

Choose plants with as many seasons of interest as possible. With trees this is particularly important; look for spring flowers, attractive fruit, autumn colour, fascinating bark and shapely branches during winter, all from the same plant. Some of the best trees include crab apples (*Malus*), birch (*Betula*) and snake-bark maples (*Acer capillipes*, *A. davidii* and *A. rufinerve*). As for cherries like *Prunus serrula* and *P.* 'Spire' – well, they have the lot!

Many flowering perennials, including coral flower (*Heuchera*), plantain lily (*Hosta*) and spurge (*Euphorbia*), have attractive leaves too. Long-flowerers like

Left: Long-lasting perennials like purple top (*Verbena bonariensis*), which flowers all summer long, should be your first choice where space is tight. This one's a magnet for butterflies too.

Above: Shrubs like Japanese snowball bush (*Viburnum plicatum* f. *tomentosum* 'Mariesii') are invaluable for flowering 'body' in a mixed border, here planted alongside *Chaerophyllum hirsutum* 'Roseum', dwarf catmint (*Nepeta racemosa* 'Walker's Low') and feather grass (*Stipa*).

Opposite: With gum (*Eucalyptus*), *Sedum* 'Matrona', *Phormium* 'Jester' and blue fescue (*Festuca glauca* 'Elijah Blue'), this harmonious scheme looks good all year round.

Verbena bonariensis should be considered, and many plants such as globe thistles (*Echinops*) and baneberry (*Actaea*) also have sculptural seedheads.

Bulbs can be grown through other plants to get two colour bursts from the same space, often at a time when there's little else around (see p122). They come in a staggering range of kiss-me-quick colours, plus they're cheap as well.

Extending the floral display

Prolong the flowering season of late summer perennials by adopting a variation on the Chelsea Chop (so-called because it coincides with the RHS Chelsea Flower Show in London). When plants are 30–40cm (12–16in) high in late spring, shorten half the shoots by one half their height; 2–3 weeks later chop back the rest. The subsequent regrowth will flower later. Also, by cutting plants back before they've flowered, you will get studier, more compact plants. Helen's flower (*Helenium*), boltonia and stonecrop (*Sedum*) love this technique but it's not suitable for those with flowers on the top of single stems, like lupins (*Lupinus*), day lilies (*Hemerocallis*) and red hot pokers (*Kniphofia*).

Designing a mixed border

A scale plan is invaluable when designing a planting scheme. To help get the spacings right, use graph paper – four squares on paper to 1 sq m (1 sq yd) on the ground works well.

To check the plants will fit, plot them on the graph paper at their size when mature, although it is normal to buy more plants than this for a closer-knit appearance to begin with (see p130). Always bear in mind the three maxims: right plant, right place; keep it simple; and less is more! Borders less than 1m (3ft) wide are common in urban gardens. In such narrow borders there may well be room for only one or two plants, so make sure they create maximum impact!

1 On the graph paper start by plotting the position of plants that you want to retain. Then plot the structural shrubs, setting taller ones towards the back, or the middle if the bed is viewed from all sides. Put a larger shrub (*eg* an evergreen one or a deciduous shrub partnered with a shorter evergreen) towards the back every 4–6m (13–20ft), depending on size at maturity. This divides the area into little bays, which are easier to work than tackling the whole border all at once. Ornamental grasses and squat evergreen shrubs – here *Artemisia* 'Powis Castle' and sage (*Salvia*) – are also important structurally, so position these now too.

2 Plot the key focal points with their strong form, to draw the eye, and the feature plants to set the style or theme. In this example I'm using easy-care shrub roses. Don't add too many, though; one, perhaps two, per bay is more than enough.

3 Accent plants come next, positioned to complement, but not clash with, the key feature plants. I like to repeat informal drifts of them throughout, for impact. The success of an accent also depends on the plants that accompany them for contrast; plot these at the same time. Here I have partnered *Allium hollandicum* 'Purple Sensation' with *Geranium himalayense* 'Gravetye' to hide its untidy stems.

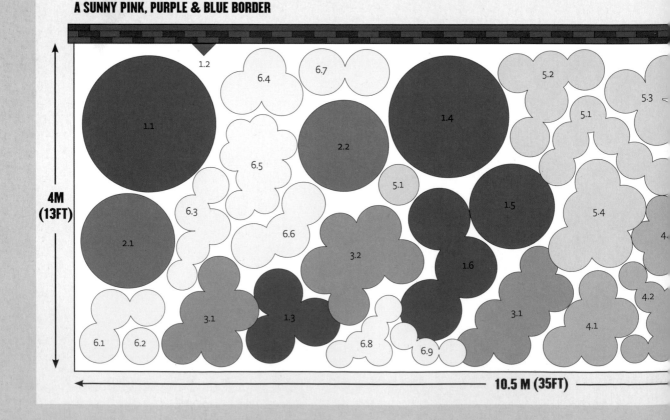

A SUNNY PINK, PURPLE & BLUE BORDER

4M (13FT)

10.5 M (35FT)

4 Now it's time for the 'infill'. Start in one area with a group of three to four different plants (if there's room) next to what you've already plotted. Work outwards, with height in mind. Try to arrange plants according to when each will be at its best, planting winter or spring shrubs next to summer perennials, for example. With smaller or slim perennials and grasses, use groups of three plants or more for maximum impact.

5 Now work on a similar-sized grouping next to the first, noting how each group works together. Make changes if necessary. Continue working in small groups like this until the first bay is fully plotted.

6 Plot the bay next door. Repetition is important for a coherent look, so it's worth repeating similar combinations, though perhaps in different densities, particularly in the foreground. Continue from one bay to the next until you're happy. Finally lay tracing paper over the plan and shade or colour in the plants that look good in each month to make sure that there is continuity of interest throughout the year. Tweak accordingly.

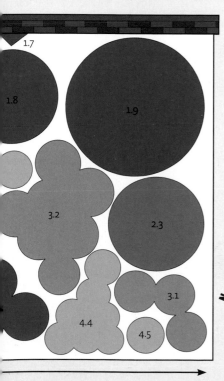

SCALE 1:50

LOCAL CONDITIONS
- fertile, free-draining soil
- pH 6.5
- full sun

KEY TO PLANTING

▬ 1 STRUCTURAL 'BACKBONE' PLANTS

1.1 *Osmanthus* x *burkwoodii*
1.2 *Clematis* 'Niobe' (on wall)
1.3 *Artemisia* 'Powis Castle'
1.4 *Callicarpa bodinieri* var. *giraldii* 'Profusion'
1.5 *Rosmarinus* 'Miss Jessopp's Upright'
1.6 *Salvia officinalis* 'Purpurascens'
1.7 *Clematis* 'Polish Spirit' (on wall)
1.8 *Myrtus communis* subsp. *tarentina*
1.9 *Philadelphus* 'Belle Etoile'

▬ 2 KEY FEATURE PLANTS

2.1 *Rosa* Munstead Wood ('Ausbernard')
2.2 *Rosa* Gertrude Jekyll ('Ausbord')
2.3 *Rosa* 'Charles de Mills'

▬ 3 ACCENT PLANTS

3.1 *Allium hollandicum* 'Purple Sensation'
(with *Geranium himalayense* 'Gravetye')
3.2 *Iris* 'Dusky Challenger'

▬ 4 INFILL PLANTS (STEP 1)

4.1 *Sedum* 'Matrona'
4.2 *Nepeta racemosa* 'Walker's Low'
4.3 *Agastache* 'Blackadder'
4.4 *Astrantia* 'Roma'
4.5 *Thymus pseudolanuginosus*

▬ 5 INFILL PLANTS (STEP 2)

5.1 *Monarda* 'Prärienacht'
5.2 *Verbena bonariensis*
5.3 *Foeniculum vulgare* 'Giant Bronze'
5.4 *Knautia macedonica*

▬ 6 INFILL PLANTS (STEP 3)

6.1 *Sedum* 'Matrona'
6.2 *Thymus pseudolanuginosus*
6.3 *Thalictrum aquilegiifolium*
6.4 *Verbena bonariensis*
6.5 *Agastache* 'Blackadder'
6.6 *Knautia macedonica*
6.7 *Foeniculum vulgare* 'Giant Bronze'
6.8 *Astrantia major* 'Claret'
6.9 *Nepeta* 'Walker's Low'

Laying out & planting a mixed border

Mid- to late autumn and early to mid-spring are the best times for planting; however, on light soils you can plant during winter. Container plants can be planted all year round (when the soil's not frozen or waterlogged) but they'll need watering regularly in summer.

1 Ensure the soil is weed-free by digging it over to the depth of a spade blade. Then add a bucketful of compost per 1 sq m (1 sq yd) to condition the soil and improve drainage. Use a fork to break up large clods, then rake the surface level; aim for a finish resembling small marbles and breadcrumbs. Lightly shuffle over the area to remove large air pockets and prevent subsidence.

2 By making reference to your planting plan, place the plants into position, best 'face' forwards. For container plants remove the pot, scrape off surface weeds before teasing out a few roots so that they grow out into the surrounding soil.

3 Plant the structural shrubs, grasses or perennials first as their position is key; you can adjust the others to fit around them. For trees and large plants don't dig deeply in the bottom of the hole. Doing so could cause the plant to sink and suffocate when the soil underneath settles. However, do prick the sides with a fork, to encourage roots to stretch out laterally (essential with clay soils). If you're planting into an existing border, where you can't dig over the whole area, a wide shallow hole at least three times the width of the pot or root system is best.

4 Position the plant in the centre of the hole and note the distance from the top of the roots to the edge of the hole; the aim is to plant at the same level as in the pot, with the uppermost roots covered by no more than 1cm (½in) of soil. For larger specimens, use a bamboo cane laid flat across the hole and measure down from that. For bare-root trees, shrubs and roses, plant to the same depth as before – look for the old, dark brown soil stain (called the nursery line) low on the stem – or cover the uppermost roots with 2.5cm (¾in) of soil.

Above: Vigorous perennials like cranesbill (*Geranium*), red valerian (*Centranthus ruber*) and white valerian (*C.r.* 'Albus') should be carefully spaced, or they'll fight with each other for water, light and nutrients in no time.

5 Gently scrape back the soil around each plant and firm with your hands before moving on to the next plant. After inserting large plants, half backfill the hole, and then firm, before filling to the top and firming again gently, so as not to ruin the soil structure (which could lead to waterlogging). Water well, and spread a mulch layer, 7.5–10cm (3–4in) thick around plants, to conserve moisture.

How many plants?

The actual number of plants to buy depends on how vigorous each one is, how quickly you want results and the role of each plant in the design (see p118).

Structural and feature plants are always worth buying big, for impact. Size at maturity is important to consider, but don't space trees, shrubs and conifers (especially slow-growing ones) at their width when mature; otherwise in the interim you'll have lots of bare soil. However, if you plant too close, particularly with perennials, they will fight for water, light and nutrients. My rough spacing guide will help (see opposite).

Large trees, shrubs and slow-growing topiary – that is, those plants that are growing in a pot the size of a builder's bucket or bigger – can be planted as individuals. Smaller plants should be planted in odd numbers – threes, fives and sevens – for impact, unless you're planting in a really tiny space like a balcony, where one might be enough. Note: the larger the pot size, the wider the spacing needed.

Seeds should always be sown at the density advised on the packet and then be thinned out or transplanted to their final spacings when large enough to handle.

SUITABLE SPACINGS

Type of plant	Distance apart	Number of plants per sq m (sq yd)
Small, dwarf & slow-growing shrubs (*eg Lavandula angustifolia* 'Munstead')	40–60cm (16–24in)	3–5
Medium-sized shrubs (*eg Potentilla fruticosa*)	80–100cm (32–40in)	2–3
Large shrubs, shrub roses & old roses (*eg Viburnum tinus*)	120–140cm (48–55in)	1–2
Large vigorous shrubs (*eg Buddleja davidii*)	160–180cm (63–72in)	0.5 (*ie* 2 sq m/2 sq yd per plant)
Bush roses (*eg Rosa* Iceberg ('Korbin'))	40–60cm (16–24in)	3–4
Small herbaceous perennials & groundcover plants (*eg Aquilegia vulgaris* var. *stellata* 'Ruby Port')	20–30cm (8–12in)	5–9
Average perennials/grasses/ferns (*eg Stipa tenuissima*)	30–45cm (12–18in)	4–6
Large and/or vigorous perennials/grasses/ferns (*eg Acanthus spinosus*)	40–60cm (16–24in)	1–3
Hedging plants (young transplants & 'whips')	20–30cm (8–12in)	3 per 1m/3ft (6 for a double row)

Opposite: Larger specimen trees, shrubs and topiary (here *Hydrangea arborescens* 'Annabelle' and small-leaved privet (*Ligustrum delavayanum*) give a planting scheme an instant sense of maturity.

Below: Choose perennials and grasses in 1- to 2-litre pots, which are about the size of a large coffee cup/small saucepan. Such plants will grow rapidly and mature in only 3–4 years, so it's not necessary to buy big ones.

Growing climbers through trees, shrubs & hedges

This is an easy way to increase interest in small urban gardens, in which space is tight.

1 Ideally plant on the shadier flank of a large tree (but not in deep shade) so the plant wraps itself around the host as it looks for the light. In a windy spot, position the climber on the leeward side of the host plant, for protection. (For detailed advice on planting under trees see pp 206–7.) Position the climber at least 50cm (20in) away from the tree's base; don't plant up close to it as the soil will be poor. Support initial growth by bending the bamboo cane with which the climber came, at an angle of 35–45 degrees, towards the host plant.

THINGS TO CONSIDER

Young plants get swamped even by delicate climbers, so choose established trees and strong-growing shrubs. Let slow growers like strawberry tree (*Arbutus*) reach a good size first.

Vigorous climbers including kiwi fruit (*Actinidia deliciosa*) and wisteria twine like boa constrictors on steroids and are only suitable for growing up the largest trees. 'Free' climbers (those that climb without requiring support) such as ivy (*Hedera*) should be avoided.

Think about pruning and maintenance. For shrubs that need spring pruning, pick Group 3 *Clematis* like *C*. 'Polish Spirit', which should themselves be pruned back to 20cm (8in) at the same time. For hedges like yew (*Taxus*) choose climbing annuals like morning glory (*Ipomoea*); plant out after pruning in spring, then cut the hedge as normal in autumn – climbing annuals are short-lived anyway.

Avoid training evergreen climbers through sun-loving shrubs; they'll block light from reaching the host.

2 Provide twining plants with something they can grip onto easily, as they can't climb trees with tall thick trunks. Do this by driving in a short stake next to the plant, then attach wire to the stake and tie off the other end at the joint of the first tree branch. Tie loosely so it doesn't strangle the branch.

3 Tie in shoots to the wire using raffia or twist ties. If the climber is planted in a lawn, wind a plastic rabbit guard (typically used for trees) around the bottom of the plant for protection. Never use a strimmer close by or you might sever the stems.

4 Drag soil up into a circular ridge around the plant 30–40cm (12–16in) away. This acts as a reservoir, keeping water where it's needed – by the roots. Then mulch with 7.5–10cm (3–4in) of compost, to conserve moisture and condition the soil.

CLIMBERS SUITABLE FOR TRAINING THROUGH TREES, LARGE SHRUBS OR HEDGES

Name	Height/ spread	Flowering/ season of interest	Suitable hosts/partners	Notes
Clematis 'Pamela Jackman' and other cultivars	**H** 2.1–2.5m (7–8ft) **S** 1–1.5m (3–5ft)	Mid- to late spring	Crab apple (*Malus*), ornamental cherries (*Prunus*) or golden rain (*Laburnum*) to double the colour in spring, or partner with summer-flowering catalpa, pride of India (*Koelreuteria paniculata*) or deciduous camellia (*Stewartia pseudocamellia*)	Sun/semishade. Prefers limey soil. Prune to control size (if you need to) immediately after flowering so shoots can ripen in time for next year. Plant 5cm (2in) deeper than normal
Hedera helix 'Pedata' (Bird's foot ivy)	**H&S** 4m (13ft)	All year round	Medium–large trees	Smaller ivy suitable for larger trees. Prune to control size in spring if necessary
Humulus lupulus 'Aureus' (golden hop)	**H** 4–8m (13–25ft) **S** 1.5–2.5m (5–8ft)	Late spring to early autumn (foliage)	Medium–large trees	Deciduous. Bright yellow leaves. All soils and aspects, except deep shade
Hydrangea anomala subsp. *petiolaris* (climbing hydrangea)	**H** 12–15m (40–50ft) **S** 5m (16ft)	Late spring to midsummer	Medium–large trees	Deciduous. Self-climbs. Tolerates semishade. Slow-growing initially, but needs a sturdy host when mature
Ipomoea purpurea (morning glory)	**H&S** 1.8–2.5m (6–8ft)	Early summer to early autumn	Shrubs, hedges, small trees, climbing roses	Half-hardy annual. Sun, moist but well-drained soil
Lathyrus odoratus Spencer Group (eg 'Lizbeth', 'Restormel')	**H** 2m (6½ft) **S** 75cm (30in)	Early summer to early autumn	Small–medium trees, larger summer-flowering climbing or rambling roses like *Rosa mulliganii*, *R.* 'Albertine' and *R.* 'Compassion'	Hardy annual. Best sown in autumn. Sun, fertile well-drained soil
Rhodochiton atrosanguineus (purple bell vine)	**H** 1.5–2.5m (5–8ft) **S** 10–50cm (4–20in)	Midsummer to early autumn	Smaller shrubs and trees	Dark pink and purple flowers. Full sun, sheltered spot. Tender, grow as an annual in all but the warmest locations
Rosa 'Rambling Rector' (climbing rose)	**H&S** 4–8m (13–25ft)	Midsummer/ early to mid-autumn (hips)	Medium–large trees	Deciduous. Fragrant creamy white flowers. Not as vigorous as most, but needs sturdy support
Tropaeolum peregrinum (Canary creeper)	**H** 3.5m (11ft) **S** 1.2m (4ft)	Early summer to mid-autumn	Hedges, small–medium trees	Full sun, sheltered spot. Tender, grow as an annual in all but the warmest spots
Tropaeolum speciosum (flame creeper)	**H** 2.5–4m (8–13ft) **S** 0.5–1 m (1½–3ft)	Late summer to mid-autumn	Hedges, large shrubs, small trees	Needs moist but well-drained, neutral to acid soil. Full sun/part shade Half-hardy, mulch deeply

Lawns

I love a lawn. It's a cheap, multipurpose, child-friendly surface and the perfect foil to colourful planting. In a front garden it soaks up water like a sponge, helping to prevent localised flash floods, and design-wise it's useful to break up large expanses of hard landscaping.

But aren't lawns a lot of work? Traditionally there's watering, mowing once or twice a week, feeding in spring and autumn, spiking to relieve surface compaction and improve drainage, plus hard raking or 'scarifying' to remove dead grass and moss.

This level of attention isn't crucial for general-purpose lawns, but if your lawn looks the worse for wear or you find mowing a real chore then perhaps it's time for a change.

Minimising lawn maintenance
- Fiddly curves make mowing difficult, so simplify the shape and reposition obstacles such as bird baths.
- Lawn edging will reinforce the sides; it's also easier to trim the grass alongside. Sturdy steel lasts a lifetime; flimsy corrugated plastic doesn't.
- Broadleaved weeds should come out, but I rather like a lawn with daisies, so consider sparing them.
- Regular weekly mowing controls weeds and toughens the sward. But don't cut lower than 5–6 cm (2–2$^{1}/_{4}$in) in summer, perhaps leaving it longer still if you've got pets or children; close-cropped lawns dry out fast.
- To promote drought tolerance by encouraging plants to root deeper, don't water the lawn in spring or early summer.
- For a general-purpose lawn you shouldn't really need to feed at all. That said, autumn feeds are okay, being high in specific nutrients that help roots, not shoots.
- For shady or damp lawns, collect the clippings, as these can encourage moss and disease. For sunny lawns, use a 'mulching' mower, which chops the grass very finely indeed, turning it into a fertilising mulch that's left *in situ*. It also improves drought resistance.

Right: A lawn with a bold shape like this is simple to maintain, while steel edging makes it easier to trim the sides too. The edging also helps keep the look crisp and stops the gravel from spilling over the sward.

Lawn alternatives

In a small garden ask yourself if you actually need a lawn. However, paving it over is often not the answer, especially in flood-risk front gardens, so why not use low-maintenance groundcover plants like camomile (*Chamaemelum*) or thyme (*Thymus*) instead? And where there's space, why not let the far end grow long, or reseed part of it entirely, to create your own colourful mini-meadow? Wildlife and children (both young and old) will love it!

Thyme lawns

Although camomile is a favourite for non-grass lawns, thyme is a better choice, given enough sun. It's not fussy about soil acidity, is more drought-tolerant and it's less

Opposite, top: Instead of replacing a lawn with plain paving, make it more interesting by adding different-textured surface treatments (here, blue-black pebbles, smooth black basalt and painted decking).

Opposite, bottom: Gravel is a cheap alternative to grass (and paving), being easy to lay and there's little need, if any, for much cement. Importantly, gravel allows rainwater to permeate through it naturally.

Below: Perhaps the best thing about gravel is that you can plant ribbons of perennials and grasses straight into it. Here, a carpet of thyme (*Thymus*) brings an informal element to the formal design layout.

likely to develop bare patches caused by wet winters or hot summers. Thyme looks (and smells!) beautiful, and grows fast; a spring planting will see a pleasing effect by the end of summer, and in a year it should be at its full glory. See p142 for how to plant a thyme lawn.

Maintenance is simple. Just water and weed while plants establish, and give the occasional trim in spring if taller types get too bushy.

Mini-meadows

• Plugs

A neglected lawn can become a mini-meadow, but grasses will dominate and you'll find few, if any, flowers. To make a meadow in all its Technicolor glory, plant young plugs of wild flowers like ragged robin (*Lynchis flos-cuculi*), field scabious (*Knautia arvensis*), greater knapweed (*Centaurea scabiosa*), ox-eye daisy (*Leucanthemum vulgare*) and red campion (*Silene dioica*). Mow the area, removing all clippings, and plant plugs randomly 30cm (12in) apart. Water well.

• Seed

Growing a meadow from scratch has a key advantage: few competitive grasses and more flowers.

Success depends on whether the right initial mix was used. There are many different ones: from spring- or summer-meadow mixes for chalky, damp or clay soils, to specially blended and colourful 'ornamental' mixes using both native and non-native plants.

Perennial or annual mini-meadow?

Perennial meadows grow best on free-draining, poor soils, where vigorous grasses won't crowd out wild flowers. If you have rich soil and want to grow a traditional meadow, you must remove the fertile top layer in order to sow in the less-rich subsoil. In all but the smallest areas, this is dirty work and difficult without hiring a digger.

Annual meadows require rich soil, and are perfectly suitable for urban gardens, where soil fertility is usually high. They're ideal if you intend to convert a border or part of a lawn. Cornfield mixes with corn cockle (*Agrostemma*), field poppy (*Papaver rhoeas*), cornflowers (*Centaurea cyanus*) and golden corn marigold (*Xanthophthalmum segetum*) are particularly eye-catching and easy to grow. A spring sowing will result in a colourful display in only 3–4 months, often sooner.

Maintaining a meadow

Annual meadows flower very quickly, but last only a year, so need sowing repeatedly each spring. Either save the seed after flowering or buy fresh.

To help plants establish properly in perennial meadows, you have to be cruel to be kind in the first year. In year two you'll really see the results.

- **Year one**

In late spring, cut back all growth to 5–7.5cm (2–3in), to keep vigorous grasses under control and encourage wild

Left: Grass that is allowed to grow long creates a pleasing meadow effect, but the grasses will dominate. If you prefer to have lots of wild flowers, then either plant a few plugs of them or start from scratch with a special meadow mix appropriate for your soil type.

flowers to put their strength into growing leaves and roots, not flowers. Collect and compost any clippings; a mower set to its highest cut, and with a box to collect the clippings, is ideal.

In midsummer cut again down to 5–7.5cm (2–3in). Check carefully and remove all perennial weeds.

• Year two
In late spring cut the meadow; check for weeds.

• Year three & thereafter
Cut once a year down to 7.5–10cm (3–4in) any time between mid-autumn (if you like your meadow tidy) and late winter – the later you leave it, the better it is for urban wildlife.

Artificial turf

There is of course another lawn alternative that, until recently, was only whispered about in gardening circles: artificial turf. Purists might raise an eyebrow, but artificial turf requires little maintenance to keep it looking good and it's particularly useful in gardens with small children, who want to be outside all year, or in those gardens shaded by trees where real grass doesn't grow well. It's permeable too.

Essentially, artificial turf is plastic matting, but laying it is a job for a specialist – it's not as simple as just placing the matting over compacted soil.

There are many different products available to suit different budgets, but for a natural look expect to pay a premium price.

Sowing an urban mini-meadow

Making a meadow seedbed is very similar to preparing the soil for normal grass seed. On very heavy soils sow all meadow seed mixes in mid- to late spring. For all other soil types sow in early autumn; perennial meadows in particular prefer this time of year.

1 First get rid of weeds. Take care to eradicate all perennials like couch grass (*Elymus repens*). Dig out the odd one with a fork – roots and all – or use a glyphosate-based weedkiller for weedy areas. Cultivate the soil to the depth of a spade's blade; for large areas use a rotivator (from hire shops). Rake the surface roughly level, then lightly shoe-shuffle over the soil to firm, and rake again. You want a fine crumbly finish – tilth. There's no need to dig in any compost or fertiliser.

A clean seedbed is important, so wait at least three weeks for weed seeds to germinate and for any perennials to reappear and then hoe, flame-gun or spray them off. If lawn turf has been stripped away to make a meadow there's no need to wait as long, unless the grass was full of weeds.

2 Weigh out the appropriate amount of seed for the area – you'll find the application rate on the packet (here I'm using an annual meadow mix for clay soil). To make it easier to sow and identify where you've sown, mix the seed with a little dry silver sand. But don't add extra seed as this can result in weaker plants prone to pest and diseases.

Opposite: A summer mini-meadow in all its glory with perennials including white ox-eye daises (*Leucanthemum vulgare*), golden marguerite (*Anthemis tinctoria*), blue viper's bugloss (*Echium vulgare*), white yarrow (*Achillea millefolium*), yellow rough hawkbit (*Leontodon hispidus*) and yellow cat's ears (*Hypochaeris radicata*).

3 Sprinkle half the seed evenly in one direction and then the remaining seed over the top at right angles to the first. Work backwards across the area, sowing the seed in front of you so that you don't tread on the seed once you've sown it. Sow a small amount at a time and, if it helps, divide the area into square metres (yards) using bamboo canes and sow the appropriate amount in each marked area.

4 Rake the seed very gently into the soil and water well using a hose or watering can with a fine rose. If birds are likely to be a problem, stretch fruit netting taut between pegs 10cm (4in) above the ground. For sizeable sowings, where this isn't practical, use bird scarers or noisy tapes that vibrate in wind. Never let newly seeded meadows dry out, so water well in dry spells.

Making a drought-tolerant thyme lawn

If mowing the lawn has become a real chore, try a scented thyme (*Thymus*) lawn instead. No mowing or maintenance is necessary, and it looks (and smells!) beautiful. Low-growers like creeping thyme (*T. serpyllum*) and woolly thyme (*T. pseudolanuginosus*) are best.

A sunny spot and very well-drained soil are essential; in fact the drier and stonier the soil, the better. It is possible to improve heavy clay soils with horticultural grit, but digging this in over a large area is hard work, and will also be expensive. If the soil is especially free-draining, plant in autumn; if not, wait until early spring.

1 Get rid of all weeds. One or two can be dug out with a fork, removing as much root as possible, but if the area is badly infested with perennial weeds, kill them off with a weedkiller containing glyphosate. If your design is in a lawn, or is a replacement for one, strip off the turf and compost it.

2 Before preparing the soil wait two weeks to check no weeds reappear; hoe them off if necessary. Fork over the area to the depth of a spade's blade, adding one bucketful of horticultural grit and one bucket of crumbly compost per square metre (yard). Break up any large clods of soil, and rake level to a fine tilth.

3 Gently shuffle over the soil to remove air pockets and stop subsidence later on. Then rake out your footprints. No additional fertiliser is necessary, especially if you've mixed in some compost; in rich soil, thyme tends to grow long and leggy.

4 Lay out each thyme plant on the soil at the correct spacing. Plants in pots 7–13cm (2½–5in) wide can be spaced 15–25cm (6–10in) apart, but bigger plants (in 1-litre/¼-gallon or 2-litre/½-gallon pots) should be placed 30–40cm (12–16in) apart. Insert each plant into the soil, making sure its rootball is just covered with soil. Firm gently.

5 Water plants thoroughly and monitor them over the next few months, watering well in dry weather. Every autumn brush off any leaves. Low-growing varieties don't need to be cut, but taller varieties will stay bushier if given a shearing after flowering. For larger areas use a mower *without* a roller and with the blades set as high as possible.

Above: In a sunny, free-draining spot a thyme lawn is a good alternative to grass. Use one species alone for a bold shock of colour, or mix different thymes together for a patchwork-like effect. A thyme lawn won't take foot traffic, so consider adding stepping stones or gravel paths.

OTHER EVERGREEN CARPETING GROUNDCOVER PLANTS SUITABLE AS LAWN ALTERNATIVES
(PREPARE THE SOIL & PLANT AS A THYME LAWN, SEE OPPOSITE)

Name	Aspect	Foot traffic?	Notes/Spacing
Ajuga reptans (bugle) and cultivars	Semishade/ shade. Moist but well-drained soil. May tolerate poor soils	Never/Rarely	Could be invasive. Set 20–25cm (8–10in) apart if plants are in 1-litre (¼ gallon) pots or in pots 13cm (5in) wide
Chamaemelum nobile 'Treneague' (lawn camomile)	Full sun. Prefers acid soil. Avoid very dry or heavy clay soil	Light (keep traffic to a minimum in the first year)	Set 10–20cm (4–8in) apart if plants are in pots 7–9cm (2½–3½in) in diameter. Don't walk on area for at least 10–14 weeks after planting
Hedera helix (English ivy) and cultivars	Full sun/deep shade. Tolerates all soils	Rarely	Could be invasive. Variegated cultivars dislike deep shade
Mentha pulegium (pennyroyal)	Sun/semishade. Prefers moist soils – don't dig in grit unless the soil is prone to waterlogging	Light/Moderate (keep traffic to a minimum in the first year)	Set 15cm (6in) apart if plants are in pots 7–9cm (2½–3½in) wide. Strong peppermint scent when crushed – ants hate it. Toxic if ingested. Classified as vulnerable by the International Union for Conservation of Nature (IUCN)
Prunella vulgaris (self-heal)	Sun/semishade. Tolerates poor soils once established	Never/Rarely	Set 15–20cm (6–8in) apart if plants are in pots 7–9cm (2½–3½in) wide; or sow seed. Rich food source for bees
Sagina subulata (Scotch moss)	Full sun/semishade. Tolerates all except very dry soil. Prefers clay	Moderate (keep traffic to a minimum in the first year)	Grows no more than 1–2cm (½–¾in) high. Plant plugs 15–20cm (6–8in) apart. Very popular in the US. *Sagina subulata* var. *glabrata* 'Aurea' is golden-coloured
Trifolium repens (white clover)	Sun/semishade. Tolerates very poor soils (but needs to be kept moist)	Rarely/Light	Treat as a temporary lawn. Sowing density 5–20g per sq m (¼–¾oz per sq ft). Rich food source for bees. Nitrogen fixer – useful green manure

Green roofs & living walls

Green roofs and living walls really make an impact by bringing a wonderful tapestry of colour and texture where you least expect to see it. They also have significant environmental benefits, from cleansing the air to reducing heating costs.

Fitting a large living wall or green roof on your house or garage is a job for a professional, because it has more to do with structural engineering than gardening. It is, however, possible to create a small-scale one yourself.

Green roofs

Green roofs can be grouped into three, depending on the depth of growing medium and the plants to be included. Both semi-intensive and extensive systems can be fitted onto gently sloping shed roofs, log stores, bike racks or even wooden bin 'boxes'.

• Intensive green roofs

These are essentially roof gardens as we know them, complete with trees and shrubs grown in deep containers or raised beds. They need looking after in the same way as any other container plantings (see the Container Gardening chapter for more details).

• Semi-intensive green roofs

In these, a layer of compost, 10–20cm (4–8in) deep, is spread over a roof. The compost is deep enough to grow perennials, but not trees or shrubs. Plants take up to two years to establish. Regular weeding, watering, feeding and possible replanting during this time are essential.

• Extensive green roofs

These are made using mat-forming or creeping plants grown on a layer, 5–15cm (2–6in) deep, of lightweight inorganic perlite, sand, rockwool – even crushed tiles and concrete – rather than soil or compost. Extensive green roofs are the most common option as maintenance is minimal once established, and being the lightest, they are best if you want to convert an existing

roof. If plants have been selected with the aspect in mind, then nothing but occasional watering and a bit of spot weeding is necessary .

Layers

A typical extensive green roof is layered like a sponge cake. The impermeable waterproof layer protects the roof; above it comes the insulation coat, then a drainage/water-storage layer on top. Made of rigid plastic and looking like the bottom half of an egg box punctured with holes, this top layer encourages excess

Above: A semi-intensive roof with snowy woodrush (*Luzula nivea*) and sweet woodruff (*Galium odoratum*) retrofitted onto a shed (with extra support installed inside to take the weight) like this is a haven for wildlife.

water to drain away while helping retain some water for dry spells. It also protects the layers underneath from damage. Above all these is a thin, semi-permeable filter sheet, which prevents the three layers underneath becoming blocked with compost; it also acts as a root barrier. Finally comes the growing medium and the plants. A frame, 10–15cm (4–6in) deep, secured around the outside of the roof, helps hold everything in position.

Specialist companies sell everything together as a package, including suitable plants commonly grown on a mat that you simply roll over the top and cut to fit.

Semi-intensive green roofs are constructed in a similar way, although a thicker layer of lightweight multipurpose compost, 10–20cm (4–8in) deep, is spread over the roof; this is deep enough to support taller grasses and perennials, but not trees and shrubs. Plants generally take up to two years to establish. During this time regular weeding, watering and a twice-

yearly feed of general-purpose fertiliser is essential. Gaps are common too, so you might need to replant if any plants fail.

The big difference in the construction of semi-intensive and extensive green roofs is that, due to the extra depth of growing medium in the former, a deeper frame of planks 20cm (8in) wide is necessary. Also a grid of wooden 'cells' (like square honeycomb) is commonly built over the whole roof to stop the compost from slipping down the slope.

Weight matters
It's unlikely a normal shed would be strong enough to support a green roof by itself, particularly a deeper semi-intensive one; most need strengthening. One option is to reinforce the shed frame inside, with stout timbers; another is to build a 'hat' on the top of the shed, supported with posts concreted in on the outside, to bear the load.

Check with a chartered structural engineer or surveyor about the load-bearing potential of your roof. For large green roofs, planning permission might also be required.

Above: Green roofs are particularly useful to soften and mask the appearance of bin stores, bike storage or garden sheds. This green roof with sea thrift (*Armeria maritima*), stonecrop (*Sedum*) and houseleeks (*Sempervivum*) would need little maintenance once established.

Opposite: Green roofs (here a shallow extensive roof planted with different stonecrops) can be used to great effect on contemporary architecture. They aren't just for traditional or cottage-garden designs.

ENVIRONMENTAL BENEFITS OF GREEN ROOFS & LIVING WALLS

Food and shelter for birds and insects

Air filtration and cleansing

Noise reduction – plants absorb sound rather than reflect it

Insulation – green roofs and living walls 'blanket' buildings, helping to cut down on energy loss

Cooling buildings – plants don't soak up and store heat, whereas bricks and mortar do retain warmth

Flood control – green roofs and living walls absorb water and slow surface runoff, helping to reduce localised flooding

PLANTS FOR GREEN ROOFS

There are hundreds of plants suitable for green roofs in either sun or shade but most share one key characteristic: drought tolerance. Here is just a small selection.

EXTENSIVE GREEN ROOFS

In sun

- *Acaena macrophylla* (New Zealand burr)
- *Armeria maritima* (thrift)
- *Aurinia saxatilis* (gold dust)
- *Euphorbia cyparissias* (Cypress spurge)
- *Raoulia australis* (New Zealand scab)
- *Saxifraga* x *urbium* (London pride)
- *Sedum acre* (common stonecrop)
- *Sedum album* (stonecrop)
- *Sedum rupestre* (stone orpine)
- *Thymus serpyllum* (creeping thyme)

In semishade

- *Ajuga reptans* (bugle)
- *Anemone nemorosa* (wood anemone)
- *Asarum caudatum* (Western wild ginger)
- *Asplenium trichomanes* (maidenhair spleenwort)
- *Corydalis lutea*
- *Duchesnia indica* (mock strawberry)
- *Mazus reptans* (creeping mazus)
- *Polypodium vulgare* (common polypody)
- *Sagina subulata* var. *glabrata* 'Aurea' (golden Irish moss)
- *Vancouveria hexandra* (American barrenwort)

SEMI-INTENSIVE GREEN ROOFS

In sun

- *Allium flavum* (yellow-flowered garlic)
- *Allium schoenoprasum* (chives)
- *Chiastophyllum oppositifolium* (lamb's tail)
- *Erigeron karvinskianus* (Mexican fleabane)
- *Festuca glauca* (blue fescue)
- *Helictotrichon sempervirens* (blue oat grass)
- *Origanum majorana* (sweet marjoram)
- *Stipa tenuissima* (feather grass)

In shade

- *Asplenium scolopendrium* (hart's tongue fern)
- *Blechum spicant* (hard fern)
- *Convallaria majalis* (lily of the valley)
- *Epimedium pubigerum* (bishop's mitre)
- *Epimedium* x *versicolor* (bishop's hat)
- *Geranium phaeum* (dusky cranesbill)
- *Liriope muscari* (lilyturf)
- *Luzula nivea* (snowy woodrush)

Right: Access to green roofs on buildings for maintenance is difficult so it's essential to choose the right plants for the location. Plants like stonecrop (*Sedum*), houseleeks (*Sempervivum*) and yarrow (*Achillea millefolium*) are the perfect choice for this exposed sunny spot.

Above & Right: In this living wall the plants, including hart's tongue fern (*Asplenium scolopendrium*), asarabacca (*Asarum europaeum*), blue fescue (*Festuca glauca*) and plantain lilies (*Hosta*), have been carefully selected with its shady aspect in mind. Note the gorgeous contrast of leaf form and texture (**above**), and how the wall forms a beautiful backdrop to the terrace (**right**). It could be masking an ugly boundary too.

Living walls

A green wall can either be a simple planting of climbers, wall shrubs or trained fruit, or a more complex engineered system, using all manner of high-tech gizmos from hydroponic mats to automated irrigation systems. On a smaller scale at home, specially designed modules or pockets filled with compost are ideal. They're easy to handle and quick to install (see p154). Maintenance is pretty straightforward too.

Importantly, always pick plants with the orientation of the wall in mind, as the climate can differ enormously (see opposite). Look after plants as you might any other container planting (see p194).

PLANTS FOR LIVING WALLS

Prostrate, low-growing shrubs, ferns, perennials and grasses can all be grown in living walls, as long as they don't have invasive tendencies. It's also possible to add fruit and vegetables for a display that really is good enough to eat!

ANNUALS, PERENNIALS & GRASSES

Sunny walls (more than half a day of summer sun)

- *Ceratostigma plumbaginoides*
- *Erigeron karvinskianus* (Mexican fleabane)
- *Euphorbia myrsinites* (spurge)
- *Festuca glauca* (blue fescue)
- *Helianthemum nummularium* (rock rose) and cultivars
- *Helictotrichon sempervirens* (blue oat grass)
- *Jasione laevis* (sheep's bit scabious) and cultivars
- *Nepeta racemosa* 'Walkers Low' (catmint)
- *Origanum laevigatum* (marjoram) and cultivars
- *Origanum vulgare* (wild marjoram) and cultivars

Shady walls (less than half a day of summer sun)

Note: Given plenty of water, all will tolerate a sunny position

- *Ajuga reptans* (bugle) and cultivars
- *Bergenia cordifolia* (elephant's ears) and cultivars
- *Brunnera macrophylla* (Siberian bugloss) and cultivars
- *Carex morrowii* 'Variegata' (sedge) and other cultivars
- *Cornus canadensis* (dwarf cornel)
- Ferns (*eg Asplenium trichomanes, Blechnum spicant, Polypodium vulgare*)
- *Heuchera* 'Can-can' (coral bells) and other cultivars
- *Hosta* 'Ginko Craig' (plantain lily) and other cultivars
- *Pachysandra terminalis* (Japanese spurge)

FRUIT, VEGETABLES & HERBS

Sunny walls (more than half a day of summer sun)

- Basil
- Cherry tomatoes
- Chives
- Coriander
- Oregano
- Purslane
- Sage
- Strawberries
- Thyme

Shady walls (less than half a day of summer sun)

- Alpine strawberries
- Lamb's lettuce
- Lettuce
- Mizuna
- Parsley
- Red giant mustard
- Rocket
- Runner beans, dwarf
- Spinach

Climbing high

For creating the easiest (and cheapest) living wall, climbers are hard to beat. Choose plants that flower at different times to get two periods of interest from the same space, or pick another climber that flowers at the same time for brilliant complementary colour or contrast. Climbing roses partnered with clematis are a classic duo. You can even pair climbers with tall hedges, large shrubs or open spreading trees (see p132).

• Free climbers

So-called free climbers need no support and therefore little maintenance. Ivy (*Hedera*) climbs using aerial roots, while Virginia creeper (*Parthenocissus*) has suckers to adhere to the surface. Free climbers often spread rapidly and are useful to cover larger areas. However, you need to consider plant vigour carefully; these climbers are tricky to control once they get going.

• Twining climbers

Twiners such as wisteria have winding stems to pull themselves up; grapevines (*Vitis*) and clematis use twining tendrils or leaves. All need trellis or stout wires for support. Don't scrimp here. Healthy climbers grow fast, and mature plants are very heavy. Substantial support is essential right from the start. For modern designs, stainless-steel cables and fittings are available from specialist suppliers, and these look good with or without plants.

The tendency of most twining climbers is to grow upwards, so, if you do want them to spread out, their shoots need to be tied in regularly.

• Wall shrubs

As they don't naturally climb, wall shrubs benefit from the support of a wall. Shoots need to be tied in regularly to horizontal supports. Rambling and climbing roses (*Rosa*) fall into this group of climbers needing support.

Left, above: Evergreen and sweetly scented star jasmine (*Trachelospermum jasminoides*) is a favourite with designers for sunny walls and fences. Being fairly vigorous (but not invasive), sturdy support is essential, because this climber needs something to twine around.

Left: *Rosa* 'New Dawn' and *Clematis* 'Comtesse de Bouchaud', a popular group 3 cultivar, make a colourful combination. Having flowered in late summer on growth made in that season, such group 3 clematis need to be hard pruned to 15–30cm (6–12in) above soil level each spring. Provided this is done, they're a good partner to roses, never being allowed to swamp their hosts.

TIDY CLIMBERS & WALL SHRUBS

Sunny walls

· *Actinidia kolomikta*
· *Clematis armandii* 'Snowdrift'
· *Clematis* 'Bill MacKenzie'
· *Clematis* 'Niobe'
· *Cytisus battandieri* (pineapple broom)
· *Eccremocarpus scaber* (Chilean glory flower)
· *Itea virginica* 'Henry's Garnet' (sweetspire)
· *Rhodochiton atrosanguineus* (purple bell vine)
· *Trachelospermum jasminoides* (star jasmine)
· *Vitis vinifera* (grapevine)

Shady walls

· *Azara microphylla* (box-leaf azara)
· *Berberidopsis corallina* (coral plant)
· *Chaenomeles speciosa* 'Moerloosei' (flowering quince)
· *Clematis* 'Nelly Moser'
· *Garrya elliptica* 'Evie' (silk-tassel bush)
· *Hydrangea anomala* subsp. *petiolaris* (climbing hydrangea)
· *Pileostegia viburnoides* (climbing hydrangea)
· *Rosa* 'Zéphirine Drouhin'
· *Schizophragma integrifolium* (Chinese hydrangea vine)
· *Tropaeolum speciosum* (flame nasturtium)

Above: Evergreen ivy (*Hedera*) climbs using aerial roots, so is ideal for covering large areas out of reach. However, don't grow it up walls needing repair; the roots will dig in and only exacerbate any problems.

INFORMATION SOURCES

There's a lot of information available on how to build living walls and green roofs – some good, some bad. This is the best of the bunch.

Websites

– http://livingroofs.org
– University of Sheffield Green Roof Centre (www.greenroofcentre.co.uk)
– The Greenroof Industry Research Portal (www.greenroofs.com)
– Green Roofs for Healthy Cities (www.greenroof.org)

Books

– *Small Green Roofs: Low-Tech Options for Homeowners* by Nigel Dunnett, Dusty Gedge & John Little
– *Planting Green Roofs and Living Walls* by Nigel Dunnett and Noel Kingsbury

Making a living wall

With a little ingenuity you can fashion a vertical garden or living-wall system from scratch – I've seen one made from old wooden pallets and plastic coffee cups! However, it's easier (and cleaner!) to use a prefabricated unit specially designed for the job.

Specially designed modules, filled with compost, are ideal at home: they're cheaper to install than hydroponic mats; have few (if any) working parts that need replacing; and looking after them is no more difficult than tending a group of small pots on the patio. The two basic types have breathable felt 'pockets' or rigid plastic ones. Always choose a spot with the plants in mind before constructing any vertical garden.

1 Firm fixings are essential – compost-filled modules are heavy when wet. Using a tape measure, mark the location of the fixing holes, and with a spirit level ensure the holes – or the product itself if you're holding it up – are level. Modules can either be fixed directly to a wall or, if you can get a good strong fixing, to a wooden fence (felt pocket systems are best for fences, as they are not flat). Alternatively secure to wood or steel battens, which are screwed into the wall behind. These help the wall to breathe and make it easier to level up each unit. To determine whether battens are required, and for working out the appropriate spacing, follow the instructions supplied with your particular system.

2 Using the appropriate bit, drill a hole and screw in (with wall plugs if need be) some wall anchors or M8/M10 coach bolts. Line up the fixing slots in the module to the bolts, and hang. If the system is being fixed to a fence, hold up each module, then screw through the eyelets with large wood screws. Tighten all fixings. Repeat if you're hanging more than one module. All systems specify the distance required between each module, so be sure to check that you have followed the instructions correctly.

3 The messy bit is next, so lay some tarpaulin on the ground beside the wall. With some systems, drainage material is necessary, so check the instructions. If required, fill the base of each module with 2–4cm (1¾–1½in) of lightweight expanded clay granules, or fine gravel. Then add compost, filling to halfway. I use two parts peat-free multipurpose, one part leaf mould and one part John Innes No. 3. Mix in slow-release bonemeal or blood, fish and bone at the rate specified on the packaging. Alternatively apply controlled-release fertiliser, which will provide nutrients when plants require them most, and you don't need to reapply them every 2–3 months.

5 Time to plant. Start at the top of the module and work downwards, so that compost doesn't fall onto the plants below. Remove each pot; pop the plant in and backfill with compost to just below the lip, making sure that the rootball is completely covered. Afterwards firm the compost and water well.

4 Arrange the plants. For complete coverage, trailing plants like ivy (*Hedera*) should be positioned at the lip of each pocket, cell or trough, so they tumble down to meet the plants growing up from below. Bushier ones can go wherever you like. For some systems, small plants are preferable to large as it's easier to firm them in. Try to achieve a relatively full look straight away by spacing plants closer together than normal. You can sow seed directly into most modules, but this means looking at ugly plastic or felt for months before the seed has germinated and plants have filled out.

6 Some systems have a built-in irrigation pipe that can be rigged up to an automatic timer; others need to be watered by hand. If there isn't a tap close by, go for a product with a built-in reservoir. Whatever system you have, though, be sure plants don't dry out. In sunny spots this might mean watering once or twice a day, especially during the growing season.

Below: Given enough water, a living wall created with plants this size will hide the black woolly pockets used here within five or six months.

Above: The gravel, smooth blue-black paving and stacked stone in this modern design beautifully complement each other as well as the planting, which includes *Skimmia japonica* 'Rubella', common box (*Buxus sempervirens*) and *Photinia × fraseri* 'Red Robin'.

Planting with stone, gravel or water

Out of all the different materials that work well in urban gardens, stone, gravel and water have such an intimate relationship with plants that they need special focus.

Natural stone

Stone can be used in many ways, from bold features or focal points to seemingly incidental natural groupings. What works best depends on the look you want, ease of access and how you might use the stone. For example,

big smooth boulders make a fantastic contrast of form to upright grasses – plus, they're great impromptu seats and climbing features for children.

Using informal groups of natural stone in the garden is often associated with alpine plants. Result: the rock garden, but rock gardens are difficult to pull off in a small urban garden, because for a natural look you need lots of space, big rocks or boulders and a slope, not just a lonely mound of soil! Where space is tight, a scree bed made of gravel and pebbles to represent the base of a rock face is a better option, although it too can look odd if isolated and not integrated into the rest of the design. For this reason it's sometimes easier to grow alpines in pots and between paving. Vigorous types like aubrieta do well at the front of free-draining beds and borders.

Above: In designs that evoke a natural setting, larger boulders, pebbles and gravel should be one and the same – just arranged with the differing heights in mind, as you'd expect to find in nature.

Design rules for natural stone

- Local stone enhances a sense of place – and it's always cheaper than stone sourced from afar.
- Rounded, water-worn boulders, stones and pebbles look better in an urban setting than imported stone.
- For a natural look, never mix different rock types.
- Use the biggest-size stone possible.
- For naturalistic arrangements, group large rocks in the centre with smaller ones around the outside.
- Don't dump large stones on top of the soil – instead, bury their bottoms. Larger rocks or boulders should be buried deeper than smaller ones.
- Try to mimic natural strata lines – keep them running horizontally just like you'd find in nature.
- Gravel and pebbles should be of the same stone.

Below: Big boulders or blocks of stone make sculptural features and are essential for a natural look, but stone this size will be heavy and awkward to shift, so consider access carefully before including it in your design.

WHAT IS AN ALPINE?

Alpines are small deciduous shrubs, conifers or perennials originating from mountainous regions. Most are low-growing and have small hairy or succulent leaves adapted to moisture loss. Although small in size, they're big on character, plus they're tough, being tolerant of poor soils, biting winds and freezing temperatures.

They are perfect for exposed terraces or balconies or sunny, free-draining slopes. The only real caveat is their need for good drainage, especially over winter.

Above: Being drought-tolerant, diminutive alpines such as houseleeks (*Sempervivum arachnoideum*) can be grown in smaller containers than normal without fear of them drying out fast.

Gravel

As pioneered by gardener Beth Chatto, growing in gravel is cheap, cuts maintenance in half and is perfect for gardeners struggling with poor dry soil. Gravel is a versatile material too, offering textural contrast with smooth paving or decking, and it is suitable for traditional and modern gardens alike.

Gravel works particularly well as a lawn replacement in front gardens, where low maintenance is preferable. The crunchy sound when walked on is useful for security too.

A sunny spot and free-draining, sandy or gravelly soil are important if you are to grow Mediterranean and coastal plants like silvery lamb's ears (*Stachys byzantina*) and glaucous-green globe thistles (*Echinops*) – an essential part of the gravel-garden look. If you have a thick clay soil or high water table, however, think twice. Digging in a lot of horticultural grit for drainage would be necessary. And gravel-garden plants look odd in wet places, where the surrounding plants are vigorous and lush. In wet zones embrace the opportunity to grow jungly, moisture-loving rhubarb (*Rheum*) and ligularia instead.

The best time to plant in a gravel garden is early spring. Young Mediterranean plants hate sitting in winter wet, so never plant in autumn.

Design rules for gravel

- Gravels come in red, grey, black, even bright white. If planting extensively, choose something neutral that will blend in; golden shingle, small rounded pebbles and weathered slate work well (although the last can be sombre en masse).
- Aim for a ratio of two thirds plants to one third gravel. Otherwise, you have a beach. Evergreen perennials, shrubs and conifers are particularly important.
- Choose a gravel size of 1.5–2cm ($^1/_2$–$^3/_4$in). Anything larger is hard to walk on, and plants will struggle to push up through it. Anything smaller and the gravel will spill everywhere or get dragged inside underfoot. If you have acid soil, avoid limestone chippings. As a guide, two bags of gravel, each of 25kg (55lb), are needed to cover 1sq m (1sq yd) to a depth of 5cm (2in). A white bulk bag from a garden centre or builders' merchant holds 1cu m (35cu ft) and covers 20–22sq m (24–26sq yd).
  Note: bound gravel (gravel mixed with clay) or resin-bound gravel isn't suitable for planting.
- Where gravel meets a lawn, install an edge or you'll be forever picking gravel out of the grass; it'll also blunt mower blades. Bricks, granite setts or logs are common edging materials. Timber edging is cheap. Metal edging creates a crisp look.

Opposite: While gravel is most commonly used in sunny spots, neutral colours can work well in semishade. While it's uncommon to mix different types, this design makes a feature of, and embraces, the artificial nature of this thin stream, by lining it with slate paddlestones. However, they don't clash with the gravel on either side.

Right: Neutral-coloured, water-worn stone and gravel are soft underfoot and, I find, suit most urban settings perfectly. Note here the healthy ratio of plants – including ferns and dead nettle (*Lamium maculatum* 'White Nancy') – to gravel, as well as the arrangement and size of the stones.

Water

We've already looked a lot at water from a design perspective but here let's look closer at the plants.

Water plants are grouped into three categories depending on where they grow best. For a sustainable wildlife pond, try and include a healthy balance of all categories, aiming to cover some 50 percent of the water with plants.

• Marginal plants

These grow on the margins of a pond, their roots reaching 5–20cm (2–8in), but no more than 30cm (12in), into the water. In deeper ponds it's usual to include a ledge for them. It is possible to plant marginals in soil, but, if you have a concrete or plastic pool, you should use special pond baskets filled with aquatic compost.

• Aquatic plants

Deep-water aquatics can grow in water 30–150cm (12–60in) deep. Waterlilies (*Nymphaea*), for example, root at the bottom of the pond, but have their leaves and flowers on the surface. Lower containers gradually so that the leaves always float on the surface. Submerged 'oxygenators' also come into this group. They float in the water and are essential for pond health.

- **Bog plants**

These plants like very damp, but not permanently waterlogged soil, growing naturally on boggy fringes of ponds or streams. However, with a man-made pond in a dry part of the garden, the area around the outside of the pond will be unsuitable for bog plants. You could extend a butyl liner further than the pond itself and bury it deeply to provide a suitable growing environment (puncture it a few times for drainage).

Below: The larger the pond the better, but even a small pond such as this becomes a magnet for urban wildlife. Depth is all-important. To suit the majority of plants and wildlife, a depth of 20–60cm (8–24in) throughout the pond is best.

POND PLANTS

Bog plants
- *Aruncus dioicus* (goatsbeard)
- *Iris sibirica* (Siberian flag iris)
- *Lobelia cardinalis* 'Queen Victoria'
- *Matteuccia struthiopteris* (shuttlecock fern)
- *Osmunda regalis* (royal fern)
- *Primula denticulata* (drumstick primula)
- *Primula florindae* (giant cowslip)
- *Rodgersia podophylla*

Marginal plants (preferred planting depth in brackets)
- *Calla palustris* (bog arum) – 5cm (2in)
- *Cyperus papyrus* (Egypt paper rush) – 20–30cm (8–12in)
- *Eriophorum angustifolium* (common cotton grass) – 5cm (2in)
- *Glyceria maxima* (water grass) – 15–20cm (6–8in)
- *Mentha aquatica* (watermint) – 10cm (4in)
- *Narthecium ossifragum* (bog asphodel) – 2–5cm (^{3}/$_4$–2in)
- *Pontederia cordata* (pickerel weed) – 10–15cm (4–6in)
- *Zantedeschia aethiopica* 'Green Goddess' – 15–25cm (6–10in)

Deep-water aquatics (max. planting depth in brackets)
- *Aponogeton distachyos* (water hawthorn) – 50cm (20in)
- *Ceratophyllum demersum* (hornwort) – n/a (submerged aquatic)
- *Hottonia palustris* (water violet) – n/a (submerged aquatic)
- *Nelumbo lutea* (American lotus) – 60cm (24in)
- *Nuphar lutea* (yellow pond lily) – 1.5m (5ft)
- *Nymphaea alba* (white waterlily) – 90 cm (34 in)
- *Nymphoides peltata* (water fringe) – 60cm (24in)
- *Orontium aquaticum* (golden club) – 50cm (20in)
- *Ranunculus aquatilis* (water crowfoot) – 90cm (34in)

Below: Don't be afraid to go it alone with only one or two pond plants, especially in geometric rills or raised pools, where many different plants would look odd and might mask the reflections on the water's surface.

Making a gravel garden

A gravel garden can be created in one of two ways. The first is more suitable for front gardens or for gardeners with little time, because it keeps weeds down and stops perennials freely self-seeding. With the second way, plants can spread more widely and therefore look more natural. It's also easier to add extra plants later with this method.

OPTION 1: THE LOW-MAINTENANCE METHOD

1 Mark out the shape of each planting bed using handfuls of dry sand. Naturalistic sweeping curves look best. Edge each bed with bricks, setts, timber or steel edging, as I've done here. In spring fork over each bed, to a spade's depth, breaking up large clods as you go, then rake it level. On very sandy soils, also dig in some compost. Shuffle over the top gently, to consolidate the soil and remove large air pockets.

Then apply slow-release fertiliser like blood, fish and bone at the rate specified on the packaging. Lightly rake it in and water well in dry weather. For paths that will get used daily, a sturdy footing is necessary. Dig down about 10cm (4in) and compact a 4–5cm (1½–2in) layer of hoggin or crushed hardcore.

2 Lay permeable landscape fabric over the area to be planted, cut to fit and pin down securely with large wire staples. Overlap the edges of each sheet by 30cm (12in) so weeds don't come up through the joints.

3 Cut small, cross-shaped slits in the landscape fabric where each plant is to grow, then plant through these as normal (see p128). The larger the rootball, the larger each slit needs to be.

4 Spread a layer of gravel, 4–5cm (1½–2in) deep, on paths and around plants, taking care not to cover low ground cover. Water the whole area well.

Right: The beauty of making a gravel garden without using permeable landscape fabric is that the plants spread naturally and self-seed where they want – all part of the charm for me.

OPTION 2: THE NATURAL METHOD

This method doesn't use landscape fabric on beds and borders, so does initially result in a few more weeds. However, this isn't a problem because plants like weed–suppressing thyme (*Thymus*) and lamb's ears (*Stachys byzantina* 'Silver Carpet') are allowed to spread freely.

Mark out, cultivate and edge each bed as before. Again, for paths that will be walked on daily, dig down about 10cm (4in) and compact a 4–5cm (1½–2in) layer of hoggin or crushed hardcore. After planting, spread a 4–5cm (1½–2in) layer of gravel on paths and around plants. Timber sleepers or stepping stones are useful to delineate the path from the planting and also provide a study footing.

SHRUBS & CONIFERS FOR GRAVEL GARDENS – HOT DRY SITES

- *Ceanothus thyrsiflorus* var. *repens* (creeping blueblossom)
- *Cistus* (rock rose) species and cultivars
- *Juniperus scopulorum* 'Skyrocket' (Rocky Mountain juniper) and other cultivars
- *Lavandula angustifolia* (lavender) and cultivars
- *Perouskia* 'Blue Spire' (Russian sage)
- *Phlomis italica* (Balearic Island sage)
- *Pittosporum tobira* 'Nanum' (Japanese mock orange)
- *Rosmarinus officinalis* (rosemary) and cultivars
- *Santolina chamaecyparissus* (cotton lavender)
- *Yucca gloriosa* (Spanish dagger)

Grow your own

Above: Just because practicalities such as easy-to-access paths and durable surface materials are at the heart of the productive garden doesn't mean it can't still be a beautiful space as well.

Few urban gardeners have the perfect plot but even with just a windowbox on a shady balcony it's still possible to have a healthy slice of *The Good Life*.

Deciding on which varieties to grow depends on how much space there is, your skill level and what you actually like to eat. Easy-to-grow, pricey crops that taste better when picked fresh should be your first choice: courgettes, strawberries, Swiss chard, cherry tomatoes, currants, spinach, salad leaves, salad onions, broad beans (you just must grow these!), runner beans and early potatoes. Modern varieties with proven drought- or disease-resistance are worth using, while traditional 'heritage' varieties are good to grow as your confidence increases, but they do need more tender loving care.

Raising crops from seed isn't difficult and helps keep down costs. However, most nurseries stock young plants you can grow on. Just remember to keep tender crops such as aubergines, courgettes and tomatoes under cloches until all danger of frost has passed.

Fast-growing radish, rocket, coriander and baby 'cut-and-come-again' salad leaves take up virtually no space at all. Tuck them in around the feet of bigger, slow-maturing brassicas, leeks and parsnips early in the season – they'll be eaten well before they get in the way.

Specially bred 'mini-veg' varieties are perfect for tiny gardens (and pots), and many mature much earlier than normal varieties (see box, opposite). It is possible to grow some bigger varieties closer together than normal to get tasty baby veg; I've done this for years. However, you must harvest leafy crops regularly.

For a continuous supply, sow little and often every 4–6 weeks. As one crop is exhausted you'll have another ready for picking. Alternatively sow different varieties of the same crop; most have early and late varieties.

Above: With a little ingenuity it's possible to grow your own, anywhere! In shallow plastic guttering this size, compact leafy crops or cut-and-come-again saladings will give the best results.

Below: Even in the smallest windowbox, hanging basket or 'planting pocket' on your kitchen windowsill it's possible to grow handfuls of tasty produce such as these tomatoes.

EASY VEGGIES FOR BEGINNER GARDENERS

· American land cress (spicy and delicious)
· Baby salad leaves
· Courgettes (the flowers are edible too)
· Garlic
· Nasturtiums (all parts of the plant are edible)
· Parsley (pour warm water along the seed drill before sowing to help germination)
· Radish
· Rocket
· Spinach ('Mikado F1' and 'Tetona' are less likely to run to seed or 'bolt' in dry weather)
· Spring onions

SPECIALLY BRED, EASY-TO-GROW, COMPACT CROPS

· Beetroot 'Doro', 'Doston', 'Pablo'
· Broad bean – 'Stereo', 'The Sutton'
· Carrot – 'Bambino', 'Little Finger', 'Parmax', 'Sugersnax'
· Courgette – 'Bambino', 'Eight Ball', 'Supremo'
· French bean – 'Ferrari', 'Purple Teepee', 'Speedy', 'Stanley'
· Marrow – 'Bush Baby'
· Pea – 'Avola', 'Reuzensuiker', 'Tom Thumb'
· Runner bean – 'Hestia', 'Minnow'
· Salad onion – 'Apache', 'Savel', 'Shimonita'
· Turnip – 'Atlantic', 'Tokyo Cross'

Crops in pots

A vegetable patch is a luxury in a small garden, but it's still possible to grow fruit and vegetables in containers. Just remember to water regularly (particularly strawberries and tomatoes) and to feed crops when they require it.

For annual herbs and veg, good-quality, peat-free multipurpose compost will do. For permanent plantings of shrubby herbs, fruit and perennial vegetables (excluding globe artichokes, cardoons and Jerusalem artichokes – they're too big), use loam-based compost.

Aubergines & chillies

Aubergine 'Pot Black', 'Baby Rosanna' and striped green 'Baby Kermit' are perfect for containers. Position one in the centre of a big tub and partner with chives (*Allium schoenoprasum*), sage (*Salvia*) and clumps of purple basil (*Ocimum*) around the outside for a delicious eye-catching display. Chillies are good too; dwarf varieties like 'Chenzo', 'Prairie fire', 'Apache' and 'Loco' don't reach more than 60cm (24in) high. To stop plants laden with fruit from toppling over, provide support with a bamboo cane discreetly positioned in the centre.

Herbs

Rosemary (*Rosmarinus officinalis*), sage, thyme (*Thymus*) and annual basil, coriander (*Coriandrum*) and tarragon (*Artemisia dracunculus*) need sun. Lemon balm (*Melissa officinalis*), chives, mint (*Mentha*), parsley (*Petroselinum crispum*) and marjoram (*Origanum*) don't mind a little shade.

Only short-lived annuals require regular watering, sometimes daily. Keep the others drier, but never let them dry out completely. Don't feed too often – even basil – as plants grow leggy and lose flavour. Also remove flowers to intensify the flavour.

Potatoes

Containers should be at least 40cm (16in) deep and wide. Potato bags, half-barrels – even dustbins – are ideal. Choose salad or early potatoes, as these mature quickly and have less top growth than maincrop varieties and therefore don't take up too much space. The varieties 'Rocket', 'Swift' and 'Charlotte' are delicious and easy. Simply place 3–5 'chitted' (sprouted) tubers on a 15cm (6in) layer of compost. Once shoots are 15–20cm (6–8in) high, cover with more compost, to prevent the potatoes turning green. Repeat over the coming months. Harvest the potatoes from early to mid-summer.

Left: Many crops look as good as they taste, and it's even possible to elevate the status of fruit and vegetables, simply by growing them in attractive pots. Large containers can also accommodate beautiful combinations.

Opposite: Willow planters – essentially low 'screens' – are useful to cover ugly plastic pots and growing bags if you want to keep up appearances but minimise costs. They come in a range of different sizes.

Above: Anyone can grow cut-and-come-again salad leaves – it couldn't be easier. Supermarket leaves are very expensive, so growing them yourself will save a fortune.

Runner beans

A favourite for larger planters (at least 40cm/16in in diameter), runner beans are easy plants to grow and suffer few pests and diseases. Colourful traditional varieties like stringless 'Polestar' or 'White Lady' trained up a pyramid of bamboo canes or hazel sticks produce the heaviest yields and look good too. Sow seed 5cm (2in) deep in individual pots on a sunny windowsill and plant out once there is little risk of frost. Or sow direct in early summer. Pinch out the tips when they reach the top of supports, and harvest when the pods are 15–20cm (6–8in) long.

Salad leaves

Mixed salad leaves (try 'Saladini', 'Misticanza D'Insalate' and 'Niche Oriental'), rocket and spinach are simple to grow as baby 'cut-and-come-again' crops, as are loose-leaved lettuce like 'Little Gem' and 'Red Salad Bowl'. To do this, scissor off the leaves 8cm (3 $^{1}/_{2}$ in) above the ground when they reach 12–15cm (5–6in) high. Cut with care, always leaving the growing points.

Strawberries

Line a hanging basket, 35–40cm (14–16in) wide, with moss, then half fill with good-quality, peat-free compost. Insert 4–5 plants through the sides, add more compost to the top, then plant another 3–4 before watering in well. Perpetual varieties like 'Mara de Bois' and 'Aromel' are best. Alpine strawberries 'Mignonette' and 'Baron Solemacher' grow well in deep windowboxes. Strawberries also do well in growing bags, troughs and tubs.

Tomatoes

Tumblers like 'Minibel', 'Lizzano', 'Gartenpearle' and 'Hundreds & Thousands' are brilliant for baskets. The variety 'Micro Tom' can be grown in coffee cup-sized pots and may produce 40–50 tomatoes from each plant!

Siting veg & fruit plants

To help crops establish quickly, start them off in little pots or modules on a sunny windowsill before transplanting out into their final position.

Fruiting and 'hearting' vegetables, including cauliflower, courgettes, tomatoes, and peppers, need a sunny spot. Leafy vegetables like lettuce, shiso, parsley,

Above: In semishade leafy vegetables (here including kale 'Nero di Toscana' and lettuce 'Green Frills') won't be as big as those grown in full sun, but they're worth a try provided you give them enough water and fertile, free-draining soil.

coriander and spinach don't mind some shade; most actually prefer cooler conditions during the summer. Fruit normally found along the woodland edge won't mind a little gloom either – try rhubarb, currants, gooseberries and, if you have room, raspberries and blackberries too.

In deep shade, only quick-to-mature salad leaves will yield results (if grown in a container or grow bag). Avoid growing under dense trees, particularly conifers – it's too dark and dry underneath.

Fruit

Big fruit trees and bushes are difficult to grow in small gardens, but it is possible to save space by growing fruit tight against walls and fences. Fruit such as apples, pears, currants and gooseberries can be grown as single-stemmed cordons (trained to grow at 45 degrees, not vertically, so the plants put their energy into flowers and fruit, rather than shoot growth).

Apples and pears are also grown as elegant espaliers, where the branches are trained into 3–4 horizontal tiers, while more vigorous plums, cherries, figs and tricky-to-grow peaches and apricots are shaped into attractive flat fans. Both have real sculptural qualities and don't need a wall for support; you can tie them to freestanding, post-and-wire supports to divide up one garden space from another – an edible boundary.

Pollination is an important consideration with fruit trees; many varieties are sterile, needing other trees nearby that flower at the same time to pollinate them. If you have room for only one tree, and there aren't any trees in neighbouring gardens, grow self-fertile varieties like 'Cox Self Fertile' apples, 'Stella' cherries, 'Victoria' plums and 'Concorde' pears.

Family trees

These have two or three cultivars grafted onto the same tree, so are also ideal in small gardens – you get different varieties that crop at different times in very little space. Apples are most common, but 'family' plums, pears and cherries are available too. Size isn't the only advantage, though. Family trees are self-fertile – each cultivar pollinating the other – so it's doesn't matter if there aren't any other trees in close proximity. A family tree is also useful as a pollinator for other varieties you might have that aren't producing fruit.

Right: Any vertical surface can be used to grow top fruit, and few climbers or living walls are this productive. Just make sure you match the plant to the particular aspect. The dessert apples here need a sunny wall to crop well.

EASY FRUIT FOR TRAINING
SUNNY WALLS (MORE THAN HALF A DAY OF SUMMER SUN)

- Dessert apple – 'Beauty of Bath'
- Fig – 'Brown Turkey'
- Pear – 'Doyenné du Comice'
- Plum – 'Victoria'
- Sweet cherry – 'Celeste'

SHADY WALLS (LESS THAN HALF A DAY OF SUMMER SUN)

- Black currant – 'Ben Lomond'
- Cooking apple – 'Bramley'
- Gooseberry – 'Invicta'
- Red currant – 'Rovada'
- Sour cherry – 'Morello'
- White currant – 'Blanka'

Below: Trained fruit (here a double 'U' cordon apple) is always grafted onto different rootstock, which determines the eventual size of the plant. Ask the supplier to check you're getting the right-sized tree for your plot. For small gardens, dwarfing or semidwarfing rootstocks are best.

The nitty-gritty of growing veg

Soil

Healthy soil means healthy crops. Dig in lots of home-made compost or a proprietary soil improver (failing that, peat-free multipurpose will do) every autumn or early spring, to improve soil structure and fertility; in very heavy clay soils this is essential. Avoid walking on wet soil so you don't compact it. With poor soil, grow your crops in raised beds (see p174) or in pots filled with potting compost.

Watering

Regular watering makes the difference between high yields and weak spindly plants. Never let the soil or compost dry out completely. Leafy veg, strawberries, tomatoes, aubergines, pumpkins and beans need watering every day in hot spells, more if grown in pots.

Above: Salad crops are particularly thirsty and may well need watering once, even twice a day in hot weather to stop them running to seed (known as bolting).

Feeding

Building up soil fertility takes time, so apply a general fertiliser like growmore or blood, fish and bone in spring; and use either for crops in pots. Most fruit and vegetables don't need regular feeding thereafter.

Tomatoes, aubergines and chillies are the exception; from about 3–4 weeks after planting, apply liquid tomato feed every two weeks.

Rotation

Crop rotation refers to groups of the same vegetable types that are moved around your garden so they are not grown on the same piece of land year after year. This rotation stops pests and diseases building up and uses some plants to feed the soil for those that follow: for example, legumes 'fix' nitrogen in the soil for follow-on hungry brassicas. Usefully it also groups plants that have similar needs, making them easier to look after.

The three rotation groups are: legumes & onions (beans, peas, onions, garlic, shallots, leeks); brassicas (cabbage, kale, cauliflower, calabrese, broccoli, Brussels sprouts); and 'roots' (potatoes, beetroot, carrots, parsnips, swede and turnip; celery and sweetcorn too).

Slot in salads, courgettes, squash and pumpkins wherever there's room. With three beds you can grow each group every year as follows:

	Bed 1	Bed 2	Bed 3
Year 1	Legumes & onions	Brassicas	'Roots'
Year 2	Brassicas	'Roots'	Legumes & onions
Year 3	'Roots'	Legumes & onions	Brassicas
Year 4	Legumes again and follow as before	Brassicas again and follow as before	'Roots' again and follow as before

Pest & diseases

If you have a really tiny plot don't obsess about crop rotation too much, just try to move brassicas and onions around to avoid club root and onion white rot.

For more detailed advice on pests and diseases see p220.

Opposite: With more than one raised bed (ideally three), practising good crop rotation is easy. Simply rotate each group (as featured above) around them each year. Because each bed is a self-contained unit you can adjust the soil pH or fertility levels to match the crop too.

Making a raised bed on concrete

Although wooden raised beds should be placed on soil, it is acceptable to build them on slabs of concrete or paving – useful for a paved or concrete-covered courtyard. Pressure-treated planks, 15–20 x 2.5cm (6–8 x 1in), are perfect for the frame. Alternatively, use scaffold planks (with the metal bands cut off); paint them with ecofriendly preservative so they last longer.

1 Mark out each bed on the ground with a tape measure to check it's going to fit comfortably. For beds you can access from both sides, the maximum width should be 1.5m (5ft). Those you can get to from only one side should be no more than 90cm (2¾ft) across; if they are wider than this, it'll be difficult to reach across without stepping on, and eventually compacting, the soil. Paths between beds should be a minimum of 60cm (2ft) – or 1.2m (4ft) for wheelchair access.

2 Carefully measure out what size works best. One 15cm (6in) plank like this makes a bed deep enough for salads, courgettes, chilli peppers, spinach, radishes, herbs and strawberries, but not for taller brassicas, runner beans, sweetcorn and roots such as swede, potatoes and tapered maincrop carrots. To grow these you'll either need to place one plank on top of the other for a deeper bed or, to keep compost costs to a minimum, grow these in deep tubs or half-barrels instead.

3 Cut the planks to size. For a raised bed laid on a concrete base, drainage is even more important than normal. Therefore, drill drainage holes in the sides, 4cm (1½in) up from the bottom of the frame, 25–30cm (10–12in) apart, using a flat spade bit, 1–2cm (½–¾in) wide. Then fix the corners together, using treated pegs of 5 x 5cm (2 x 2in) or fence posts of 7.5 x 7.5cm (3 x 3in) cut 1cm (½in) shorter than the total board height. Screw together using decking screws 4–5cm (1½–2in) long. Always keep checking the frame is square, as you work, using a carpentry square.

4 With the frame in position, add 3cm (1in) of small gravel and broken terracotta crocks to help with drainage. For raised beds on soil, the layer of drainage material isn't necessary (nor are the holes in side for that matter).

5 Fill the bed with compost. A mix of 70:30 loam-based John Innes No. 3 and good-quality, peat-free multipurpose compost is ideal. A blend such as this should never need replacing provided you add a little garden compost and a sprinkling of general fertiliser like blood, fish and bone in early spring and midsummer, to top-up fertility levels. For deep beds you might need to buy tonne bags of screened topsoil. Be mindful that the deeper the bed, the more growing media you'll need, and the greater the expense. Rake the soil level and then gently shuffle across it to firm. Rake again to remove your footprints and then start to dig in your plants. Water well after doing so.

CONTAINER GARDENING

Containers offer all the beauty of the bigger garden, but in miniature. They're manageable and versatile – great for beginner and experienced gardeners alike – plus they can bring welcome cheer to a garden almost instantly, regardless of the season.

For many gardeners, notably those with balconies, roof terraces or concrete-covered courtyards, containers essentially are the garden, and plants are the only way to hide the featureless grey. But nowadays containers aren't just somewhere to nurture vibrant spring and summer bedding or special tender plants. Trees, shrubs, even fruit and vegetables can be successfully grown in them, the latter giving you fistfuls of fresh produce right outside your door.

With design in mind

In today's urban garden, containers are also highly valued from a design perspective. Positioned cleverly, pots add emphasis and frame doorways, arches or special views and vistas. They can also help break up a large patio, defining the dining space from the lounging area – without completely cutting one off from the other and the rest of the garden. Big containers – those larger than 40cm (16in) – can be sculptural features or fantastic focal points in their own right. If they're particularly attractive they don't even need to be planted.

I love containers for their flexibility and how they allow you to experiment with planting combinations and design. You can move them around as the seasons change and plants are at their best or, if you tire of the arrangement, shuffle them into new positions for a brand-new view. They're also great to liven up a planting scheme when there's a lull in colour – pop in a pretty pot and you'll have instant colour. And what's more, because you get to pick the compost, you can grow what you like, regardless of local soil conditions.

Opposite: This modern oval planter, here filled with culinary favourites like rosemary (*Rosmarinus*), thyme (*Thymus*) and variegated sage (*Salvia officinalis* 'Tricolor'), is the perfect permanent home for herbs.

Right, top: Containers are ideal for combinations of colourful annuals and bulbs, which might otherwise get lost in beds and borders. They can easily be moved into more prominent positions when at their best too.

Right, below: Containers don't always need plants. Attractive pots by themselves make wonderful focal points or, in this case, water features.

Design rules

Style & setting

The setting, notably the building in which you reside, together with the design style determine what looks best. Deep muddy bronze COR-TEN troughs and brightly coloured columns planted with feathery grasses or clipped topiary balls look cool and contemporary. Weathered lead planters and ornate wirework baskets crammed with winter cyclamen suit traditional settings.

Above: Containers spaced like this bring a formal note to a garden and can help to define one space from another. Here the planting (including *Narcissus* 'Thalia' and *Muehlenbeckia complexa*) has a softening effect, but it takes a secondary role to the pots themselves.

For grand designs choose giant stone urns; woven willow baskets and textured terracotta are suitable for more intimate surroundings.

Grouping & placement

Cottage-inspired designs are relaxed, so informal collections work best here. In gardens with strong geometry, containers should be used for their architectural impact, because seemingly random arrangements can look odd. They should be placed prominently by themselves or else the same pots and plants should be repeated like soldiers on parade, where they can be used to enhance linear features, such as steps and paths, or provide invaluable safety devices on the edge of a patio or deck.

Above: Contemporary cubes complement the geometric layout of this roof garden and also forge links with surrounding architecture.

Right: Containers with plants such as these diminutive auricula primulas need to be grouped for impact. As plants come into flower they can readily be moved into position. When pots are set close together they're easier to water too.

I find the view from the building particularly important here. If a lone container is designed to be a focal point, then it should be positioned clearly to catch the eye from the main sitting area. Similarly a formal procession of identical pots shouldn't obstruct the view; they should be orientated to embrace it.

Harmony & repetition

Try to avoid combining too many different styles and materials – stick to one or two. A limited palette will stop the cluttered mess so common with collections that have evolved over time or through necessity.

Small pots (less than 40cm/16in high) of bulbs or herbs often look lost by themselves, so for greater impact group them together or plant more than one with the same thing.

Scale & size

Consider the size of the pot (and plants) in relation to the rest of the garden. If the container has a significant design role, think big. Small gardens certainly don't need small pots; perversely they'll actually have the opposite effect and shrink the garden further still. Big pots are long-term features, not to mention heavy to shift. To check the proportions are right, sketch over photographs to visualise how they might look *in situ*. Alternatively fashion a life-size model using cardboard boxes (see pp76–7).

Container-grown plants are thirsty beasts so the bigger the container the better, because the compost won't dry out so quickly and there'll be plenty of compost for roots to spread. Admittedly the plants themselves need consideration – small alpines require shallow bowls, for example – but the greater the volume of compost, the more plant roots will be protected from temperature extremes. However, teeny plants in huge containers don't work. The excess compost will be prone to waterlogging.

Other practical factors will also have an influence. In front gardens use large weighty pots, which can't be stolen easily. On balconies and roof terraces weight matters too, but pots need to be as light as possible. In exposed windy spots avoid tall slim containers as these tend to blow over.

The container itself

The container is every bit as important as the plants – in some designs even more so, with plants taking a secondary role.

- Bold shapes are best for impact.
- Containers with detailed pattern need a simple palette of plants. Colourful mixed plantings work best in simple pots.
- If in doubt choose pots with classic shapes and neutral colours – one reason why terracotta is popular.
- The container should also complement the planting for a harmonious look (see pp188–9).

Right: Less is most definitely more. This sculptural combination makes a dramatic focal point, and the COR-TEN steel container continues the semi-industrial theme of the design.

Above: These beautiful stone urns, partnered with Iris 'Action Front', might cost more than many other materials, but they bring a timeless elegance to a garden design.

Materials

Whatever your budget or personal taste there's a pot to match it. But while aesthetics are important, a key consideration – often forgotten – has to be how the particular material dictates when and how much you need to water.

TERRACOTTA (CLAY)

- Always buy frostproof terracotta; there's nothing more disappointing than seeing the base of a pot shell off or the sides just crumble. Note: 'Frost-resistant' doesn't mean the same as 'frostproof'!
- To hurry the weathering process along, paint live yoghurt mixed with a bit of manure on the sides. Given a little shade, the pot will look positively ancient in no time.
- Terracotta's natural porosity is beneficial for plants because it's good for drainage and allows air to the roots; however, in dry weather it also soaks up water from the potting compost, leaving plants parched. To stop this, discreetly line the inside with sheet plastic (leaving drainage holes uncovered) or use with rigid plastic liners.
- Before planting, soak new terracotta pots in a bucket until the clay is saturated.

GLAZED TERRACOTTA

- Single-colour glazes look better with mixed plantings.
- Check the glaze when you buy, especially if lining up identical containers together as the finish can differ, depending on where they were positioned in the kiln.
- Always buy frostproof.
- Pots with a crackle glaze and those unglazed on the inside are susceptible to frost damage. Sometimes water seeps under the glaze, which then starts to flake off. Solution: line with plastic, as before.
- Less porous than unglazed terracotta, so are great for smaller pots.

STONE – NATURAL STONE

- Heavy and expensive.
- The perfect choice for classic designs as it ages beautifully.
- 'Picked' granite and smooth slate pots are available for modern schemes.
- Age natural stone as you would terracotta (see above).

Above: Wooden barrels bring antiquated charm to a traditional setting or design and are big enough for permanent plantings of larger shrubs and trees. They make great little ponds too.

STONE – CAST OR RECONSTITUTED STONE (INCLUDING TERRAZZO)

- Cheaper than natural stone.
- Made by mixing crushed stone with concrete or resin. Choice pots are finished by hand to look like the real thing.
- Both period and ultra-modern designs are available.

FIBREGLASS & GRP (GLASS-REINFORCED PLASTIC)

- Perfect for balconies or roof terraces.
- Currently not recyclable but very long-lasting.
- Not porous so the compost doesn't dry out, but is prone to waterlogging if there aren't enough drainage holes.

WOOD

- Hardwood containers made from oak or teak cost more than pressure-treated softwood ones, but they last longer.
- Stain, paint or varnish to suit your home or garden design.
- Origin – look for a Programme for the Endorsement of Forest Certification (PEFC) or Forest Stewardship Council (FSC) stamp on the label. This means that the timber is from a sustainable source.
- For traditional designs, old wine and whisky half-barrels look lovely.
- Expensive wooden pots usually come with a rigid plastic or metal liner, which stops water staining the outside.

METAL

- Traditional cast iron and lead age gracefully, but have been superseded by cheaper and lighter GRP imitations.
- Copper looks beautiful, especially when it oxidises.
- Vast array of modern cubes, columns, cylinders and spheres available in galvanised and stainless steel.
- Rusty COR-TEN steel planters should not be placed on light-coloured stone as the rust can bleed, staining the surface.
- Powder-coated metal containers can be painted any colour.
- Large thin steel planters can bow in the middle when full of compost, so internal supports are essential.
- Metal containers heat up in sun, which dries the compost. Use in semishade or line with 6–8 sheets of newspaper. This gives the roots a little protection, and holds onto water.

PLASTIC

- Cheap, light and maintenance-free.
- Huge polypropylene tubs, without drainage holes, can be made into tiny ponds. They don't become brittle and crack.
- Natural or neutral colours like dark granite, dull terracotta, sandstone or even dark green are preferable; alternatively hide them.
- Prone to waterlogging, so ensure plenty of drainage holes.

Choosing plants

While almost anything can be grown in a container, some plants require less maintenance than others, which makes them a better choice, especially if you're strapped for time. As growing fruit and vegetables in pots has already been looked at on pp166–7, I'm concentrating on ornamentals here.

Vigour
It's true that growing plants in containers restricts their growth and keeps them smaller than normal, rather like bonsai. But fast-growing monsters such as Boston ivy (*Parthenocissus tricuspidata*) and firethorn (*Pyracantha*) are just too much bother. You can grow trees in containers, but stick to easy-care ones such as evergreen magnolias, crab apples (*Malus*), ornamental cherries (*Prunus*), small birch (*Betula*) and snake-bark maples (*Acer capillipes*, *A. davidii* and *A. rufinerve*), which shouldn't need regular repotting.

Tolerance of exposure & drought
On balconies and roof terraces, plants with mounding or carpeting forms or with silver-hairy, thick-waxy or needle-like leaves that have naturally adapted themselves to such conditions should be your first choice. Alpines, smaller conifers, shrubs (like lavender/ *Lavandula*) and perennials (including stonecrop/ *Sedum* and autumn daffodil/*Sternbergia*) will help keep the need for water to a minimum. Elsewhere, it is not always necessary to consider a plant's suitability for a certain aspect or watering needs, particularly in a damp, shady and sheltered spot.

Temporary vs. permanent plantings
Traditional bedding such as snapdragons (*Antirrhinum*) and primroses (*Primula*) brings bright seasonal colour.

Opposite: Embrace the energy and exuberance of vigorous annuals and perennials like this Mexican fleabane (*Erigeron karvinskianus*) – combined here with *Sedum sieboldii* 'Mediovariegatum'. They'll make an impressive display quickly and are easy to manage in a container.

Right: Limiting plant choice to one or two varieties is the simplest way to create a bold coherent look. Repetition like this also creates visual harmony.

For year-round interest, displays need to be replaced once, typically twice. They need a lot of maintenance too. With this in mind, permanent plantings are preferable in the urban garden, because such architectural shrubs, clipped topiary, palms, ornamental grasses and evergreen perennials have foliage and form, which visually last a lot longer than a temporary display. Perhaps the best scenario is to have a backbone of permanent plantings, with a smattering of temporary seasonal colour from annuals and tender perennials.

Mixed displays?
One variety en masse makes a bigger statement and has more visual impact than a mixed planting, but the latter allows for creativity and a more intimate and exciting relationship between the plants – one spilling through or trailing down another, for instance.

Above: Cottage-garden penstemons need a container with rustic character to match; this weathered fruit crate is ideal.

Right: Terracotta has a natural affinity with plants. Those featured in this informal group, including *Hosta* 'Bressingham Blue', *H.* 'June', diascia, lobelia and coral flower (*Heuchera*) complement these traditional pots perfectly.

I think it all depends on the size of the pot and the plants themselves: for example, to appreciate a mixed planting using dainty cuphea, alyogyne or cussonia you need several plants and a pretty big pot, or the same design repeated close by, to make an impression. Let's not forget that you can shift pots and plants around to try a different combination the following year if things don't work out – that's half the fun!

For informal containerised displays arrange big containers with trees and shrubs at the back. Position the shorter pots and plants in order of height down to the front. Make sure you can water each pot easily.

Of course you don't need to stick to growing petite plants in low pots; you can elevate the status of smaller plants by growing them in thin columns or narrow vases.

Relationships
Decisions, decisions. The size, shape, texture and colour of the plants in the container, and their relationship to the container itself, need thought.

As well as the pot and the plants being in proportion to the size of the space, the plants should be proportional to the size of the container. A general rule of thumb is that the planting should be no more than $1^1/_2$–2 times the height or width of the pot.

For mixed displays in the same pot, tradition demands a centrepiece with striking form or foliage: try honey bush (*Melianthus major*), phormium, *Abutilon* 'Kentish Belle' or topiary lollipops. Shorter bushy frothy fillers come next – osteospermum, cranesbill (*Geranium*), asparagus fern (*Asparagus densiflorus*) and coral flower (*Heuchera*) – with smaller ornamental grasses often intermingled for contrast. Low ground cover like helichrysum, violets (*Viola*) and busy Lizzies (*Impatiens*) go round the outside to spill over the edges. Position plants towards the front of the pot if it is to be viewed from that direction.

For bold effects choose bright or contrasting plants and containers, while for something more subtle pick relaxed forms and natural or cool colours and textures.

Planting permanent pots

Permanent plantings are ideal for reliable texture, form and colour. Wide containers are best. Avoid amphora-shaped pots and those with narrow necks; when it comes to repotting in 3–4 years' time, the plant will be difficult to get out without sacrificing it or the pot.

As a guide, choose a container 7–9cm (2½–3½in) bigger than the rootball; otherwise the excess compost will inevitably get waterlogged, suffocating plant roots. If you're planting more than one plant per pot, allow for a gap of 5cm (2in) between each rootball. Pot size is less important for temporary spring and summer bedding.

1 Planting in a plastic liner (here, an old compost bag) is useful, as it requires far less effort to lift the plant from the pot when the time comes. And with terracotta it stops the clay from 'wicking' away water from the compost.

Arrange the liner around the pot sides and ensure it does not block the drainage holes at the bottom. Then spread a layer of drainage material such as broken terracotta crocks or coarse gravel in the bottom of the pot before you plant. For a pot 50cm (20in) high, the drainage material should be 5cm (2in) deep. Balcony gardeners worried about weight can use small chunks of polystyrene or lightweight clay beads as drainage material.

2 Use loam-based compost (or, for acid-lovers, ericaceous compost as I've used here), mix in controlled-release fertiliser and, to cut back on watering, some presoaked water-retaining gel, according to the instructions on each packet. Afterwards fill the pot to halfway and firm gently.

3 Now for the plant. First soak the rootball in a bucket of water, then remove the container, scrape off any weeds or moss, and tease out the roots from the rootball with your fingers – this will encourage them to grow out into their new home.

4 Place the plant centrally in the container, adjusting it until the best-looking side favours the front. The top of the rootball should be approximately 5cm (2in) below the container lip. If it looks as if the plant will be too deep, add more compost underneath to raise it up.

5 Fill around the outside of the rootball and lightly cover with compost, then firm gently with your fingers. Ensure that the rootball is covered by 1–1½cm (½–¾in) of compost so it does not dry out. Add more compost if necessary.

6 Water well, then mulch the top of the pot with composted bark. This keeps the moisture locked in and helps to stop compaction in the compost, caused by water regularly thumping down on the surface. Mulch sun-loving plants with gravel.

Potting compost & drainage

Peat extraction causes significant damage to precious wildlife habitats and natural ecosystems, so always try to buy peat-free potting composts. For temporary plantings use a good-quality multipurpose peat-free one based on shredded bark or coir.

Permanent plantings of trees, shrubs and perennials need sterilised loam-based compost – John Innes No. 3. This doesn't dry out so quickly and holds onto nutrients for longer than soilless ones. It's heavier too – perfect for exposed spots.

Acid-loving restios, camellias and rhododendrons need lime-free ericaceous compost.

For planting on balconies or roof terraces, where weight matters, use premium coir or bark-based composts as they're lighter, easier to move round and safer too.

Never throw away spent potting compost. Empty it on the compost heap or spread around established plants in beds and borders to keep weeds down. I know many gardeners who recycle compost and reuse it again; I've done it myself. However, don't incorporate more than half into the new mix, and certainly not for the same type of plant. Never reuse

if pests and diseases have been a problem, and be prepared to feed plants earlier than usual too: any nutrients will have been used up the first time around.

Good drainage is essential because container plants left sitting in water will rot or their roots will suffocate from lack of oxygen.

Always add coarse gravel or, better still, broken terracotta crocks to the bottom of a container so that its drainage holes don't become blocked with soil. As a guide, the depth of the drainage material should be about one tenth the height of the pot.

The soil in hanging baskets and wall baskets tends to dry out very quickly so they do not require a layer of drainage material.

POT MAINTENANCE

To prevent pests and diseases being passed on, it's good practice to scrub the inside of all pots thoroughly with hot soapy water before you reuse them.

Terracotta	No maintenance required.
Glazed terracotta	Wipe down with hot soapy water, using non-abrasive sponges/clothes.
Stone: Natural and reconstituted	See terracotta (above). Fingermarks are inevitable after planting. If the pot has no glaze, scrub off the marks using a gentle scourer or fine wet-and-dry abrasive paper. Test on a hidden area first to make sure you don't damage the surface.
Stone: Terrazzo	Wipe with hot soapy water using non-abrasive sponges/cloths. Remove stubborn stains and algae with a weak vinegar solution.
Wood	Normally lined to protect the wood from decay. If not, special liners are available, or use an old compost bag (don't cover the drainage holes). Prolong the life of softwood containers, woven willow and hazel with a plant-friendly wood preservative. Wipe down hardwood containers with warm soapy water, and oil if required.
Fibreglass & glass-reinforced plastic	Wipe down with warm soapy water. Avoid abrasive cleaners/ scourers.
Plastic	Wipe down with warm soapy water. Never use abrasive cleaners/scourers – scratches are impossible to repair effectively on plastic.
Metal	Wash down with warm soapy water. Buff stainless steel with window cleaner or the appropriate polish and a soft cloth – wiping on wax car polish or baby oil will stop water stains thereafter. To stop rust around new drainage holes, apply anti-rust paint, but ensure the holes remain open. COR-TEN steel planters need no care or maintenance.

Opposite, top: One of the great things about container growing is that you can pick the perfect compost to match. For acid-lovers like these *Erica gracilis* and *Calluna vulgaris* 'Alicia' use ericaceous compost.

Opposite, bottom: Gravel is useful for drainage if you haven't got any terracotta crocks. On balconies and roof terraces where weight matters use broken small chunks of polystyrene.

Right: Polished metal containers like these should need no more than the occasional wipe down with a damp cloth to keep them looking good.

Caring for container plants

Pot-grown plants are entirely dependent on you, their carer, but a little work goes a long way and the rewards far outweigh the effort. In addition to fertilisers (see pp216–17) they also benefit from the following.

Water-saving aids

Plants in containers always dry out more quickly than those grown in open ground, yet water is a precious commodity. Anything you can use to cut back the amount, and how long it takes to water, is a good thing.

- **Sponges**

In high summer, baskets and windowboxes need soaking, once, even twice, a day. To retain more water

Above: The easiest way to keep watering to a minimum is to choose drought-tolerant plants such as houseleeks (*Sempervivum*). The plant in this chimney pot won't need watering more than once a week.

in the compost place an old sponge or drip tray in the base to act as a reservoir.

- **Drip trays**

For individual containers, drip trays, which collect water, are useful. Place them under the pot, and the water they catch is then drawn up into the compost as it dries out. If matching trays aren't to be found, completely transparent versions are available, which don't detract from the pot design. Large plastic trays aren't attractive but they're useful for collections of small pots, and make watering easier.

- **Water-retaining crystals/gels**

These should be added to the compost when filling the basket or pot. They swell on contact with water, keeping more water in the compost and thus available to plants. Important: add water to the crystals before mixing them into the compost, or else they'll push both plants and compost out of the container as they swell.

- **Hessian cover**

To cool terracotta pots in dry spells and stop the compost from drying out quickly, temporarily wrap pots (not the plants) with hessian sacking and string. Alternatively use old bed sheets or bath towels.

- **Self-watering reservoirs**

These are common in large commercial containers, and smaller versions are available for home use. Essentially a tank is placed into the bottom of a container before planting. The top of its feed pipe should be just above the compost. Once a week check the float, which measures the water level, and top up as required. Alternatives based on a similar concept rely on special matting and/or a wick to draw water into the compost.

- **Automatic watering systems**

When hooked up to an outside tap, these systems deliver water to plants through a series of 'stick-in' drippers, which effectively get water to exactly where it's needed – the roots. Such systems can be automated, which is great for peace of mind, especially if you're away on holiday. The downside is that lots of snaking pipes look quite ugly; hide discreetly where possible.

Above: The containers on this small balcony contribute to the structural and spatial layout of the whole design. Such big containers can accommodate permanent plantings, which only need routine watering and feeding.

Repotting permanent plantings

Even permanent plantings will eventually exhaust themselves and crave fresh compost. You shouldn't need to repot them for at least 3–4 years, but if you find a mass of roots bursting out from the top of the pot or significant numbers poking through drainage holes in the bottom, it's time to repot your plants. Poor stunted growth and yellow leaves are warning signs too. Choose a new pot at least 7–9cm (2$\frac{1}{2}$–3$\frac{1}{2}$in) bigger in diameter and replant exactly as you did before (see p190).

Root-pruning permanent plantings

As with bonsai, it's possible to trim the roots back on established plants, so you don't continually need a bigger pot. If it's a tree, perennial or tough shrub such as box (*Buxus*), you can remove up to 30 percent every time before repotting in fresh potting compost. Do this in early spring as the weather improves.

Root-pruning does depend on the plant – those like daphne, magnolia and tree peonies (*Paeonia*), which dislike root disturbance, will hate you for it – that's why they're not usually recommended for pot-growing. But how can you be sure about others? If the plant is costly, rare or needs very particular care then I wouldn't try it.

When perennials become congested, divide them into smaller fist-sized clumps and replant. Inevitably you'll have too many to use, but never throw extras away – swap or gift them to friends and neighbours.

Planting reclaimed objects

If you want to get really creative, check out the pot potential of reclaimed and recycled objects. There's no quicker way to bring personality and instant character to your garden.

Attractive olive-oil cans, metal baby baths, wine crates – as long as they'll hold soil and allow for drainage, you can plant up these and other assorted containers. When making your selection, consider the style and theme of your garden – you don't want it ending up looking like a rubbish heap or junkyard!

1 Clean the container. For metal ones use a wire brush to scrub off any flaky rust from the inside. If the container is something you particularly cherish then treat the rust with an automotive rust killer; always wash the insides thoroughly afterwards to remove any residue. If you plan to paint the outside, sand with medium-grade aluminium oxide paper and wipe down with white spirit. If there is insufficient drainage, use a drill with the appropriate bit to create some drainage holes, 2cm (¾in) wide, in the base; space them 8–10cm (3½–4in) apart.

2 Spread a generous layer of gravel or broken terracotta crocks on the bottom. How deep depends on the container but aim for a depth that is at least one tenth of the overall container height.

3 Fill the container with the appropriate potting compost (see p192). Mix in water-retaining gel to act as a reservoir for roots, before adding controlled-release fertiliser at a rate advised by the manufacturer on the packaging.

4 Water each plant, then remove each one from its pot . Place individually into the container, positioning each rootball 2cm (¾in) below the pot lip. Add compost underneath if need be, then fill around the plants, firming gently. Spring and summer plantings are a temporary excess, so don't be frightened to cram in more plants than normal, for a bigger and brighter display.

Above: Reclaimed 'pots' might not last as long as one that has been specially made for the purpose, but they're much cheaper and come packed with bags of character.

5 Water well after planting and mulch the top with composted bark, to conserve moisture. For alpines and sempervivums use fine horticultural grit or gravel for the mulch.

FACTORS TO CONSIDER

• **Life span** – Untreated metal cans and timber fruit crates won't last longer than 2–3 years even if they're lined with plastic. These are best for temporary herb plantings or spring and summer bedding.

• **Contaminants** – Check oil drums or fertiliser tubs are clean from pollutants, which might poison the compost and your plants. This is especially important if you plan to grow fruit and vegetables.

• **Weight** – Large containers should be planted *in situ* (as always). Dragging them to their final position might scar surfaces, not to mention hurt your back.

• **Drainage** – Ensure there are holes in the base of the container. If not you'll need to make some before planting.

• **Safety** – Check for sharp edges or rusty nails or screws; file back or remove them carefully before you plant.

• **Materials** – Rusty containers might 'bleed' and stain surfaces; enamelled sinks chip easily – site accordingly.

• **Size** – Make sure potential pots are deep enough for your plants; tiny tin cans look cute but there'll be little room for plant roots to spread. For large oil drums and similar-sized containers, fill the bottom third with chunks of broken polystyrene or an upturned bucket to save on compost.

MANAGING THE URBAN GARDEN

In this book I've talked a lot about maintenance, in particular how to keep work to a minimum. This isn't because I'm lazy – and nor is this book intended only for those with five minutes a month to spare. It's just that nowadays most people never have as much time to look after their gardens as they'd like.

I recognise that not all of us want to be gardening day in, day out, either – life's too short and there's absolutely no shame in this. And if you're just starting out, why throw yourself in at the deep end, only to struggle? Instead, take your time, get to know your garden; learn to love it. You can always do more as your skill and enthusiasm grow.

Maintenance matters

Maintenance is a major consideration behind the design style you choose: the materials; how many containers there are; and the plants you grow – in short, everything. It's pointless investing time and money into a glorious garden only to watch it decline over the years, just because you weren't realistic at the beginning.

Recognising what you can do, and more importantly what you can't do, form a key part of the design process (see p16). The essence of the modern 'sustainable' garden is one that can be managed without unnecessary intervention too.

A relaxed approach is important. The gardens at famous flower shows are certainly inspirational and the perfect place to copy clever ideas, but you should view them as highly manicured stage sets. Real gardening is a little more rough around the edges.

How much work?

Gardens with a lawn, hedges, fruit and vegetables, plus lots of containers, require work – particularly during spring and summer – whereas minimalist schemes full of hard landscaping don't. If you can't spare more than an hour a month then this is the look for you. But these gardens cost more: a wall is 10 times more expensive than a hedge, for example. And for those who actually love gardening there's often not enough to do.

For me, it's about finding some middle ground – a garden with enough going on to potter in four or five times a month (or more if I want to) but not somewhere I feel constantly under pressure.

Opposite: Shrubs (here including box, *Hebe* and *Hydrangea arborescens* 'Annabelle' partnered with blue *Hosta* 'Hawaii') offer unparalleled reliability and should be the mainstay of the low-maintenance planting scheme. Note the contrasting textures of the foliage in this combination.

Right: This roof terrace, with its decking, easy-to-clean furniture and large containers planted with drought-tolerant pines (*Pinus*) and grasses, needs nothing more than a sweep every other week.

Above: Ground cover like *Euonymus fortunei* 'Minimus' won't need any work and keeps weeds at bay. When used en masse like this it complements the crisp minimalist aesthetic of the garden design.

Lawns

The easiest way to cut maintenance time in half is to replace the lawn completely, with, for example, thyme or a meadow (see p137). For tiny lawns a little extra paving is a possible solution, but for anything larger choose materials such as gravel, pebbles or clay pavers (see p156). They're cheaper, but more importantly they're permeable too, letting rainwater soak away naturally. In the front garden permeable lawn substitutes are essential – solid surfaces contribute significantly to localised flooding.

Whatever material you choose, carefully consider the size of the space as this will have a big impact design-wise. Replacing a small lawn with thyme or gravel probably won't affect the overall composition too much. On a large scale this would be a big change, though, and is best worked out on the drawing board, where the redesign or addition of other features can be considered at the same time.

Plant selection

Diverse plant collections need lots of work. Instead, your first choice should be shrubs, ornamental grasses, border conifers, bulbs, sturdy perennials like purple coneflower (*Echinacea purpurea*) and Siberian flag (*Iris sibirica*) and weed-suppressing ground cover. Once established, all need little pruning, staking, feeding or deadheading. Bedding displays and vegetable gardens in particular absorb considerable time. Plant few of these, or use big pots, which need watering less often.

Tougher alternatives are always available: substitute top-heavy *Crambe cordifolia* and delphiniums with perennials that don't need staking, such as meadow rue (*Thalictrum*) or plume poppy (*Macleaya*). Similarly, find space for shrub roses (*Rosa*), which generally avoid pests and diseases, rather than bush roses, many of which are vulnerable and need regular pruning.

Always choose healthy vigorous plants, with bright, evenly spread top growth; weak, spindly plants or those harbouring pests will always struggle to thrive. Trees should have no broken branches or noticeable scrapes on the trunk. Bulbs should be fat and firm.

Left: Unlike grass, a camomile (*Chamaemelum*) lawn path like this won't need mowing, unless it grows tall and leggy. A sunny spot and a free-draining soil are essential to stop it looking patchy.

Below: With its evergreen shrubs and perennials, including *Euphorbia* x *pasteurii* 'Roundway Titan', strawberry tree (*Arbutus*), *Libertia grandiflora* and *Pittosporum tobira* 'Nanum', this design is evidence that low-maintenance gardens can be stunningly beautiful.

Bottom: Box (*Buxus*) topiary brings a stately sculptural presence to any garden, yet any more than this number will take an age to trim. To help avoid box-blight disease, trim once in early summer when it's likely to be dry for a week, as the fungal spores thrive when it's humid and damp.

With container plants look for lots of fine feeder roots in fresh compost. Roots of bare-root plants should be well developed and not severely pruned or damaged.

Another common cause of trouble later on is poor planting technique, particularly in less-than-ideal soil and weather conditions. For best practice see pp128, 132, 140, 190, 204 and 206.

Hedges & topiary

Clipping topiary takes time, although it depends on the amount: one plant is fun; 50 are laborious. Plants with similar forms could work just as well – globular *Hebe* 'Emerald Gem' and *Pinus mugo* 'Mops' (a cultivar of dwarf mountain pine) can be suitable alternatives to box (*Buxus*) balls in a sunny spot. Instead of clipped cones, choose tidy columnar shrubs like fastigate Japanese holly (*Ilex crenata* 'Fastigata').

Restrict formal hedge height to what you can easily manage. In a garden with sufficient space, consider growing an informal hedge (where the outline of each plant is visible); these might need pruning only once every two or three years.

Planting tight to a wall

The soil is usually dry and shaded next to a house or garden wall, making these some of the worst places to grow plants. In a wide border always plant 50–60cm (20–24in) away from the wall, out of its shadow, where the soil and growing conditions are better. In gardens with only a narrow strip of soil beside a wall, it's more of a challenge to get plants to thrive.

1 Remove all weeds in the border. Then add a bucketful of well-rotted garden compost per square metre (square yard), digging or forking it into the soil to the depth of a spade blade. Take care not to damage concrete foundations; if you find any, move out to where the soil is deeper. Break up large clods of soil, firm and rake it level, aiming for a fine friable finish, or 'tilth'. If planting in spring add some blood, fish and bone or growmore and water in well.

2 Dig a hole 5cm (2in) wider than the pot, but only slightly deeper – too deep and the plant will sink as the soil underneath settles. Then carefully push a fork into the bottom of the hole to check that there are no obstructions that might stop water draining away easily – plants by walls need more water initially, and you need to ensure they won't end up sitting in a pool 20cm (8in) under the soil surface, unbeknownst to you.

3 If the plant is dry dunk the pot in a bucket of water to soak the rootball; leave it for five minutes. At the same time fill the planting hole with water and let it drain away. This will stop dry soil nearby from 'wicking' water away from the plant, just when it needs water most. I also find it useful to check that water will drain way easily.

4 Remove the plant from its pot and position it in the hole. Some gardeners prefer to tease out a few of the roots before planting, to help them grow outwards into the surrounding soil. I find you needn't bother, unless on removing the pot you discover a real mass of roots with little compost showing.

Left: When given enough water, climbers, grasses and colourful perennials such as white African lilies (*Agapanthus africanus* 'Albus') should thrive tight against a wall like this. However, don't position larger shrubs and trees in such a position, because they might undermine the foundations and destabilise the wall.

PLANTS SUITABLE FOR DRY SHADE BY WALLS

CLIMBERS & WALL SHRUBS
- *Hedera helix* (ivy) and cultivars
- *Hydrangea anomala* subsp. *petiolaris* (climbing hydrangea)
- *Parthenocissus tricuspidata* (Boston ivy)
- *Pileostegia viburnoides*
- *Schizophragma hydrangeoides*

SPREADING SHRUBS & PERENNIALS
- *Euonymus fortunei* 'Emerald Gaiety'
- *Geranium* x *cantabrigiense* (cranesbill) and cultivars
- *Polystichum aculeatum* (hard shield fern)
- *Polystichum setiferum* (soft shield fern)
- *Vinca difformis* (periwinkle)

5 With the plant in the centre of the hole, check its depth. The top of the rootball should be covered by no more than 1cm (½in) of soil. Backfill around the plant, firming gently with your hands. Water well, then mulch with 7.5–10cm (3–4in) of well-rotted compost. Expect to water the plant every week (every day in really dry spells) for six months or so.

Note: When adding fresh compost check the soil level doesn't increase too much up against a house wall. If the final level ends up being close to or above the damp-proof course, then moisture will creep upwards, causing damp walls inside. The damp-proof course is a thin black line near the base of the wall made from either slate or plastic; it prevents rising damp. Keep the soil at least 15cm (6in) below this line. In older properties make sure the soil level is also well below any airbricks. Consult a builder if advice is needed.

Planting under mature trees

Plants under trees suffer from lack of light and competition for moisture; the closer to the trunk, the worse these problems get. Large trees and low canopies exacerbate them still further. Unfortunately, nothing grows under dense evergreen trees, especially big conifers.

On the edge of a high canopy, in dappled light and deep rich soil, there will be lots of plants that'll thrive, including sizeable structural shrubs like box (*Buxus*), yew (*Taxus*), Oregon grape (*Mahonia aquifolium*) and laurustinus (*Viburnum tinus*). Close to the trunk, as conditions worsen and tree roots become thicker, choices are more limited. Here, choose tough evergreens like ivy (*Hedera*) or tenacious woodland perennials like barrenwort (*Epimedium*), glory of the snow (*Chionodoxa*) and lily of the valley (*Convallaria*). These flower in spring before the leaf canopy fills out, and die back afterwards, to re-emerge the next spring.

1 About 30cm (12in) away from the trunk, pick out potential planting pockets between the roots of the tree and lightly cultivate the soil using a hand fork or trowel, adding handfuls of well-rotted compost or manure. Avoid digging too deep, as it's easy to damage the roots. A sprinkling of general fertiliser like blood, fish and bone will help plants to establish.

2 Dig a hole twice the width of the rootball, but only slightly deeper. Always choose healthy plants, as they are more likely to tolerate these less-than-ideal conditions. Soak the rootball in a bucket of water. Fill the planting hole with water, allowing it to drain; do this twice if the soil is really dry.

3 After gently teasing out the roots from the rootball with your fingers, position the plant – here lilyturf (*Liriope muscari*) – in the centre of the hole so the top of the rootball sits just below the edge. Then backfill with the soil you've dug out, and firm gently. Small plants will establish more readily than larger ones, and are also preferable as they require smaller planting holes, which are less likely to damage a tree's roots. Of course, small plants are also cheaper, making failures less dramatic.

PLANTS FOR DEEP DRY SHADE CLOSE TO THE TRUNK OR UNDER A LOW TREE CANOPY

- *Brunnera macrophylla* 'Jack Frost'
- *Cyclamen hederifolium*
- *Dryopteris filix-mas* (male fern)
- *Epimedium* x *perralchicum* (barrenwort) and other evergreen varieties like *E. alpinum, E.* x *rubrum*
- *Euphorbia amygdaloides* var. *robbiae* (wood spurge)
- *Galium odoratum* (sweef woodruff)
- *Geranium phaeum* (dusky cranesbill) and cultivars
- *Iris foetidissima* (stinking iris)
- *Ruscus aculeatus* (butcher's broom)
- *Vinca minor* (lesser periwinkle) and cultivars

PLANTS FOR UNDER HIGH CANOPIES OR UNDER THE CANOPY EDGE

- *Aquilegia atrata* (columbine)
- *Buxus sempervirens* (common box)
- *Digitalis ferruginea* (rusty foxglove)
- *Dryopteris filix-mas* (male fern)
- *Erythronium* 'Pagoda' and other varieties
- *Polemonium caeruleum* (Jacob's ladder) and cultivars
- *Polygonatum odoratum* (Solomon's seal)
- *Pulmonaria saccharata* (Jerusalem sage) and cultivars
- *Skimmia laureola*
- *Tellima grandiflora* (fringe cups) and cultivars

4 After planting, water well, then mulch deeply around the plants with well-rotted garden compost, composted bark or, better still, leafmould; a layer 7.5–10cm (3–4in) deep is ideal.

5 Regular watering is essential throughout the year after planting. Also, keep the mulch topped up every six months – this conditions and improves the soil over time. Retain autumn's fallen leaves on the ground around where you've planted too.

Wise watering

Lack of water is the most common reason plants perform poorly, and it is the biggest killer of new plantings. Bedding, recent transplants, young seedlings, vegetables and soft fruit are particularly susceptible to drought, especially if they are grown in pots or baskets. Concentrate on these by soaking new plantings and transplants regularly for the first six months or so. Be prepared to water well for up to a year after that during spells of dry weather.

When planting, draw soil into a circular mound around each plant, firming with your hands, to create an 'earth dam'. This will prevent water running off the surface. For trees, a mound 10–13cm (4–5in) high with a 1m (3ft) diameter is appropriate; it can be less than half this height and width for shrubs and perennials.

Alternatively, with larger trees and shrubs, professional gardeners nestle a perforated flexible drainage pipe on top of the roots when planting, leaving the end above ground. Pour water into the pipe, and it will get to the roots fast. Once well established, you'll probably never need to water them again.

When planning a planting scheme also bear in mind how much water each plant is likely to need. For example, those with silvery, needle-like, downy, thick or waxy leaves such as broom (*Genista*), lavender (*Lavandula*) and rock rose (*Cistus*) have adapted to cope with little water.

The right way to water

Aim water at the roots where it's needed, to give a proper soaking. One good drench each week is best, encouraging plants to root deeply, seeking water further down. Always check you've watered enough by pushing your fingers into the soil, down to the roots. It might be wet on the surface, but dry underneath.

Watering systems are economical with water and easy to use. Perforated 'leaky' pipe and stick-in drippers (great for containers) are the cheapest options and

Right: This storm-water planter is an ingeniously creative way to recycle water. The planting, including *Iris* 'Flight of Butterflies', blue flag (*I. versicolor*) and *Euphorbia palustris*, has been chosen to cope with the wet conditions.

can be automated (some from a water butt). Check the battery and inspect the system regularly for blockages. Irrigation specialists can install professional systems, which are useful on a large roof terrace, but unnecessary elsewhere if you've matched plants with the soil and microclimate (see p105).

Ideally, you should water when the sun's at its lowest, often first thing in the morning or early evening. Never water at midday in hot sun unless plants are wilting badly and their shoots drooping to the ground; at such a time, water on the leaves will magnify the intensity of the sun's rays and may 'cook' young foliage.

Don't waste water spraying leaves, unless you need to rinse off dust in polluted areas. Therefore, ditch the sprinkler, or else focus the spray very carefully. Position a jug underneath the spray to monitor how much you're

Below: Installing a water butt is the easiest way to recycle water. Here a recycled plastic drum works a treat, but, if looks count, choose old oak barrels – just expect to pay a lot more for them.

Above, left & Above, right: In an exposed urban seaside spot these plantings of cotton lavender (*Santolina chamaecyparissus*), *Hebe albicans*, lamb's ears (*Stachys byzantina*), sea holly (*Eryngium bourgatii*) and catmint (*Nepeta x faassenii*) will not only tolerate exposure and salt-laden winds but will also not need watering by hand once established.

watering, and move the sprinkler regularly. Don't use the sprinkler on the lawn unless absolutely necessary – letting grass grow longer in hot spells helps it survive.

Conserving water

With increasingly erratic climatic conditions, water management and conservation are at the heart of sustainable modern gardening.

You should therefore collect rainwater (known as blue water) by diverting downpipes into a water butt or two. Go for old oak casks if aesthetic appeal is important or you can't hide the butt with planting. If you're doing a major redesign of your garden, consider using underground storage tanks, which can be installed before paving or a lawn is laid.

It is possible to recycle water from baths and showers (known as light-grey water), provided you use ecofriendly detergents. However, unless you install a specialist grey-water treatment filter, light-grey water doesn't keep well and can't be stored for long periods.

Organic manures and compost absorb water like a sponge, which is especially helpful with free-draining soils that typically have a high proportion of sand or silt. Dig in as much well-rotted organic matter as you can before creating a new border, and also mulch generously around established plants.

Coping with waterlogged sites

Flooding caused by run-off from too many hard surfaces is increasingly common in urban areas. Plants in waterlogged soil suffer because water fills the air spaces and both beneficial soil life and plant roots can't breathe. In the worst cases there'll be permanent puddling on the soil surface. Leaves go yellow and wilt. Roots will be black and mushy, and the soil may be mottled grey in colour and smell of rotten eggs.

Therefore, you should always keep off waterlogged soil; treading on it will ruin its structure and lead to compaction. If you must walk on it, use boards to spread your weight. Once the soil has dried out, dig in lots of compost. Thereafter, mulch regularly to protect its structure as well as enhance drainage and aeration. In persistently waterlogged soil, drainage systems installed by professionals help, although these typically need an outlet such as a ditch or swale, unless permission from the local authority is granted to empty into public drains.

Raised beds can also improve matters, but if your soil is always wet and is only made worse following heavy rain, rethink your planting scheme. Many plants including colourful and dramatic rhubarb (*Rheum*) and rodgersia thrive in boggy soil.

Water-logged lawns shouldn't be be cut until they've dried out. To improve surface drainage, stab a garden fork 10cm (4in) into the lawn every 20cm (8in) or so and fill the holes with lawn sand. For larger lawns use a wheeled or motorised aerator.

Ensure non-permeable surfaces are slanted towards borders or a lawn so the water can soak away naturally. Alternatively, replace these surfaces with permeable paving or porous ones like gravel, which allow rainwater to drain through and so help prevent localised flooding.

Left, top: To create living space in a garden with really wet soil, why not build above it with decked platforms like these. They're a low-impact, non-invasive (and therefore comparatively cheap) solution, needing minimal foundations for the legs of the supporting structure underneath.

Left: If water puddles on the surface, spiking will aerate the lawn and help relieve compaction. Do this with a fork every season. On thick clay soils prone to waterlogging also use a hollow-tine aerator, which removes larger 'plugs', every three to four years. Afterwards brush in a mixture comprising three parts loam, six parts horticultural sand and one part garden compost (or a coir-based compost if you haven't any garden compost available). This will help prevent moss too.

Garden compost

Every urban gardener should have a compost heap or bin. This means you can cut back on the amount that goes to landfill, and save yourself a fortune on the bagged stuff. By choosing the ingredients yourself you know exactly what's in the compost too.

Slugs, millipedes, woodlice, beetles and spiders are an essential part of the composting process. A few fruit flies are fine, though a big swarm might mean the compost is too wet; add drier brown material (such as prunings or shredded cardboard) to restore the balance. Ants are harmless but could mean your heap is too dry. The presence of worms is good news. They prove your heap is working properly!

Rats are attracted to compost bins for two reasons – shelter and food – but don't let them put you off the composting business. It's rare for rats to become a problem if you keep the heap moist (not wet), turn it regularly, bury food waste deep in the middle and never add dairy products or meat. A covered bin also offers more protection, and a sheet of strong weld mesh placed underneath will stop rats burrowing in. A spot some distance from the house is best for your compost bin or heap, but not so far away that you won't use it regularly.

Things you can put into a compost heap
- Prunings (not diseased)
- Vegetable peelings
- Fruit
- Tea bags
- Coffee grounds
- Grass clippings (not in big lumps)
- Spent bedding plants
- Hair
- Shredded newspaper, cereal boxes and egg boxes
- Cardboard
- Eggshells
- Old bedding hay from rabbit cages
- Wood ash (in moderation)
- Leaves (in moderation)

Opposite: Growing your own fruit and vegetables and making your own compost go hand in hand; one essentially feeds the other.

MAGIC MULCH

Mulch is wonderful material. It helps retain moisture, maintains cool soil temperatures, insulates colder clay soils, reduces compaction, minimises erosion and suppresses weeds. Organic biodegradable mulches such as garden compost, animal manures, straw and leafmould also top up fertility levels in the soil and help maintain good soil structure.

Before laying a mulch, always blitz the weeds, then water thoroughly or wait for heavy rain, because it is essential to lay the mulch over moist soil. Spread a thick layer – 7.5–10cm (3–4in) is plenty. Don't cover any foliage or bank up the mulch against plant stems, as this causes rot; leave a mulch-free gap of 3–5cm (1–2in) around the base of each plant. Apply mulches in spring, when the soil's warming up, and top it up again in autumn.

Items to avoid on a compost heap
- Plants diseased with onion white rot, potato blight and club root
- Perennial weed roots
- Plastic wrappers and labels
- Glossy magazines
- Cooked food
- Raw meat
- Dairy produce
- Fish
- Nappies
- Bones
- Dog or cat faeces
- Coal or coke ash

BOKASHI COMPOSTING

Compost on a small scale under the kitchen sink using a 'Bokashi' bin. Fill it with kitchen scraps layered with special bran full of micro-organisms, which break everything down in 10–14 days. Afterwards, you can dig the fermented mixture into a compost heap to break down further, or you can bury it in beds and borders. Unlike conventional systems it's possible to compost meat and dairy products.

Making compost

Compost is easy to make, but first get a basic bin. Garden centres and DIY stores carry a huge range, and you certainly don't need to spend a fortune. For larger gardens a makeshift affair using old wooden pallets tied with wire will do as a compost bin/heap.

Site the bin in a sunny spot if possible, discreetly camouflaged but not too far from the house, otherwise you won't use it. In a small garden where the bin will be obvious, go for a wooden model or an attractive one disguised as a beehive. Preferably, place the bin on soil, rather than on paving slabs or concrete, for drainage.

1 Add ingredients to the bin as and when they are available. Composting is like making a cake. Aim for a ratio of two thirds green material (grass clippings, fruit etc.; see p213) to one third brown (dry plant stems, egg boxes, shredded newspaper). Such a ratio prevents the mixture becoming too wet or too dry.

2 Keep all the ingredient pieces on the small side, or they'll take a long time to break down. Chop up big stems with secateurs or a shredder before adding them.

3 To stop the heap from becoming wet and smelly, don't add too much green stuff, like grass clippings, all at once. Always try to alternate layers. 5–7.5cm (2–3in) thick, of drier 'brown' material between every 7.5–10cm (3–4in) of 'green', because the brown material helps air circulate in the heap, which speeds up the composting process.

4 Although in general the compost bin can simply be left alone to let nature take its course, you can speed up the decomposition process by turning the bin contents every two weeks, with a garden fork, to introduce some air. This creates a hot heap where everything rots down more quickly. If you don't turn your heap, it'll still work, but the materials take longer to decompose, sometimes as long as 6–7 months.

5 The compost is 'done' when it looks like dark brown earth and has no obvious smell. It probably won't appear like the bagged stuff, being lumpy, sticky or full of eggshells, but that's fine; it'll still be perfectly useable. Inevitably, thick stems won't have rotted down, so fish them out and put them back in the compost bin, for further decomposition.

MAKING LEAFMOULD

Bag up leaves from deciduous trees such as lime (*Tilia*), oak (*Quercus*) and London plane (*Platanus* x *hispanica*). Then water the leaves well, if dry (this helps the composting process), poke a few holes into the sides of the bag to let air in, tie it at the top and leave the bag in a sheltered spot out of sight. In 10–12 months' time it'll be ready to spread over your garden soil.

Avoid conifers or evergreens like holly (*Ilex*) – these take ages to rot. Shred and add them to your compost heap instead. If you don't have a tree in your garden, sweep up the leaves from quiet streets before they are salted.

Left: Organic composts release nutrients more slowly than inorganic (man-made) compound fertilisers like growmore or simple fertilisers like sulphate of potash. The nutrient levels aren't as high either, which means you're less likely to over-apply and damage plants in the process.

Feeding

Garden compost and composted animal manures are excellent sources of low-level nutrients for your soil. For most garden plants it's enough to dig these in before planting, and then top up fertility levels by mulching in spring and autumn.

I haven't used separate fertilisers on established borders for 20 years – plants that grow strongly don't need it. For intensive vegetable gardens and plants showing signs of a nutrient deficiency, however, supplements are necessary. For plants growing in containers, including house plants, orchids and citrus fruit, additional feeding is essential.

Which fertiliser?

Generally, fertilisers high in nitrogen encourage leafy growth, whereas those high in potassium are for bigger flowers and fruit. Each packet or bottle of fertiliser will state its uses. Don't apply high-nitrogen fertilisers in late summer, as it will only stimulate lush sappy growth that will die in the first autumn frost.

For pretty much everything from containers to vegetables, general fertilisers such as growmore are easiest to use. These contain not only all the major nutrients but also many of the minor ones (see box left). For organic growers, choose seaweed meal or pelleted chicken manure instead. I like using blood, fish and bone as a base dressing, to help kick-start new plantings, but it contains little potassium.

NUTRIENTS AT A GLANCE

MAJOR NUTRIENTS
- Nitrogen (N) makes plants green and helps shoot growth
- Phosphorus (P) boosts root growth
- Potassium (K) enhances the size and quality of flowers and fruit, and also increases resistance to frost.

MINOR NUTRIENTS
- Calcium (Ca), magnesium (Mg), sulphur (Su), iron (Fe), zinc (Zn), boron (B), manganese (Mn), molybdenum (Mo) and copper (Cu) comprise the minor or 'trace elements'. Plants don't need them in particularly high quantities, but they're still vital for healthy growth.

Opposite: A fully functioning compost heap will provide all the nutrition you need to boost established plants. Of course, the compost will help improve drainage, nutrient retention and soil structure too.

SLOW-RELEASE, CONTROLLED-RELEASE OR QUICK-RELEASE FERTILISER?

Fertilisers come in various forms – liquid, granules and powder being the most common. Just make sure you read the instructions carefully; it's easy to do more harm than good.

- **Slow-release fertilisers** such as blood, fish and bone feed plants gradually for 2–4 months, depending on the soil type, temperature and rainfall.
- **Controlled-release fertilisers** deliver nutrients over a set time (usually six months) and are useful for containers, but they are more expensive than slow-release ones.
- **Quick-release fertilisers** (also known as fast-acting fertilisers) supply nutrients in a quick burst and usually come in liquid form. They're most useful for container vegetables or summer bedding. But don't overdose, as this leads to weak spindly growth prone to pests and diseases.

WHEN TO FEED

Temporary container displays The nutrients in standard, off-the-shelf potting compost last for only about six weeks, so thereafter water with quick-release liquid fertiliser every two weeks (I swear by tomato feed). Alternatively, work controlled-release fertiliser into the potting compost at planting time.

Permanent container plantings Use controlled-release fertiliser in spring; or feed plants with slow-release general fertiliser in early spring and again in early summer.

Vegetable gardens Mulch regularly (see p213) and dig in garden compost or manure every winter, particularly after growing potatoes, and before planting beans. Topdress with slow-release general fertiliser in early summer, to replace nutrients that have been used by spring crops

Troubleshooting in the urban garden

No garden can escape weeds or attack by a few pests and diseases, but with vigilance it's possible to keep them under control. Cultural controls such as mulching (see p213) should be the first option. Weedkillers and pesticides might yield results, but I'd stress great caution in their use; consider them only as a last resort.

Controlling weeds

The golden rule when dealing with weeds is to hit them hard and hit them early!

• Annual weeds

Chickweed (*Stellaria media*) and groundsel (*Senecio vulgaris*) are typical annual weeds, being prolific and shallow rooted, but they don't last long. Control is easy: slice off at ground level with a sharp hoe on a dry day, before these weeds set seed. Or use a gas-powered flame gun or boiling hot water, keeping both away from your precious plants. Both techniques work brilliantly on weeds in paths or permeable paving.

• Perennial weeds

These have long aggressive roots or underground bulbs/corms. You must remove all the roots, so dig them out with a fork or use a flame gun. Hoeing doesn't work as a way of getting rid of perennial weeds, although it does weaken the plants.

For a big established problem of persistent perennials such as horsetail and couch grass, the method favoured by those committed to an organic ethos is to chop such weeds to ground level and then cover the weedy area entirely with heavy black plastic, weighted down. This does kill them over time. For a severe problem a translocated (systemic) weedkiller travels through the plant, killing the roots. However, be very careful using such weedkillers around children, pets and fish. Never,

JAPANESE KNOTWEED

Identifiable by its light green, heart-shaped leaves, head-high, bamboo-like stems and creamy white flower tassels in late summer, Japanese knotweed (*Fallopia japonica*) is unfortunately common in cities. It is the very devil to get rid of. Digging isn't recommended as this breaks up the roots, spreading the problem further still. You can however treat small infestations with a weedkiller containing glyphosate, spraying in late spring, when shoots are only waist high. Be prepared to repeat the treatment for 3–4 years. Always burn – never compost – the roots and stems, and never include them with household waste. For large infestations call in experienced professionals.

ever rotivate a patch of perennial weeds in an attempt to control them; if you do they'll spread and multiply! Don't throw the roots onto the compost heap – burn them or submerge in a bucket of water, for 4–6 weeks.

Perennial weeds are most tricky to eradicate when growing among other plants. In the worst cases, dig up your desired plants, teasing out any weed roots from them as you go, before dealing with the weeds left behind. Replant beds and borders only once they're completely weed-free; this may take four months or so.

To stop your neighbours' perennial weeds colonising your plot, invest in a vertical plastic running bamboo barrier made of thick plastic. Dig it in alongside your boundary at least 45cm (18in) deep, and check for invaders regularly.

Once your garden is clear of weeds, use mulches to help prevent them coming back (see p213).

Perennial nasties

Ground elder
(*Aegopodium podograria*)

Ground elder can be spotted by its white, flat-headed flowers in late spring. This carpeting perennial spreads by underground rhizomes. Deep digging – with a little more delving 3–4 weeks later – works wonders in removing it. (Consider carefully before using translocated weedkillers containing glyphosate.)

Hedge bindweed
(*Calystegia sepium*)

This twining climber with large, heart-shaped leaves and white trumpet flowers spreads by underground rhizomes. Around established plants, persistent handweeding is the best way to get rid of it. In areas where there are no precious plants, you could use a glyphosate-based weedkiller. Never let hedge bindweed seed.

Couch grass (*Elymus repens*)

Notorious as a real pest, couch grass spreads with white underground rhizomes. Regular digging helps control isolated pockets, but for huge infestations you may need to apply glyphosate-based weedkiller. Couch grass is impossible to control in lawns. Dig over (pulling out the weed roots) or spray the entire area, then cultivate and reseed it.

Horsetail (*Equisetum arvense*)

Summer is the primetime for this very invasive perennial, with its deep roots (down to 2.1m/7ft) and upright, fir tree-like shoots. Avoid occasional shallow weeding, because this only spreads the problem. Repeated applications of glyphosate-based weedkiller might be necessary. Lightly crush the stems beforehand so the chemical can penetrate effectively.

Dock (*Rumex* sp.)

Like dandelions (*Taraxacum officinale*), docks have a deep taproot that needs to be removed. Dig them out with a thin spade or special dandelion 'grubber'. You needn't use chemicals here.

Bramble (*Rubus fruticosus*)

Because they are difficult to eradicate once established, dig out bramble plants early on, to save time later. For bigger problems, cut back growth then burn, before removing the stumps by hand (you'll need to dig deeply). Or use triclopyr- or strong glyphosate-based weedkiller; more than one application is often necessary.

Perennial nettle (*Urtica dioica*)

Nettles are relatively easy to control. Simply dig them out with a garden fork as the deep golden yellow roots don't travel deeply. Wear gloves!

Wild garlic (*Allium ursinum*)

The white umbels of spring-flowering wild garlic reach 50cm (20in) high. In the right setting it's beautiful, but wild garlic can be a nuisance elsewhere. It spreads by underground bulbs that can be dug out – sieve the soil to make sure you get each one. Never add the bulbs to the compost heap and don't dig in autumn as you'll spread the dormant bulbs.

Above: Beer traps, copper slug rings, crushed seashells, hair, bran and wood ash spread around susceptible plants can work well as slug and snail traps and barriers, although a little experimentation is usually necessary. You don't need to use slug pellets containing metaldehyde, which is toxic to animals.

Above: Birds love soft fruit such as red currants, white currants and especially strawberries. Netting suspended above susceptible crops (not simply laid over the top) will stop them ravaging your crops.

Identifying pests & diseases

Pests and diseases are inevitable, especially if you grow lots of fruit and vegetables, which don't have natural resistance to common foes.

For information and help in identifying pest and disease problems in the garden, I would recommend *RHS Pests and Diseases* by Pippa Greenwood and Andrew Halstead. Every gardener should possess a copy of this excellent book.

Treating pests & diseases

If you do find that you have a problem with a pest or disease, try to tackle it with biological controls or natural alternatives such as pesticides based on fatty acids or fish oils, instead of resorting to noxious synthetic controls straight away. However, for most gardeners nowadays pesticides and fungicides are used as a last resort; prevention is always better than cure.

Always act early to stop problems escalating. Removing the first signs of attack – pinching off the odd infected leaf for example – might be all that's necessary.

Guarding against attacks

Happy plants are healthy plants, which are less susceptible to attack, so don't allow the soil around plants to dry out or neglect to feed them. Good hygiene also pays dividends. Thoroughly clean seed trays, pots and pruning equipment, use sterile compost and dispose of infected material. Encourage natural predators too. Piles of leaves attract slug-munching

slowworms and hedgehogs. Bird feeders entice garden birds, which are partial to caterpillars and greenfly, as well as snails.

Slug problems? Beer traps and copper slug rings work; slugs and snails get an electrical charge as they try to slime over them. Scratchy eggshells or coarse sand spread around plants can also be effective.

Simple barriers work wonders in protecting plants from pests and diseases. Thin floating crop covers such as enviromesh, laid loosely over carrots, cabbages, strawberries and soft fruit, are particularly effective for their respective pests. Always remove the cover while plants are flowering.

Certain plants are reputed to be great companions to others if grown close by. Some supply nutrients, while others attract beneficial natural predators or may act as a deterrent to pests or diseases. Dill (*Anethum*) and fennel (*Foeniculum*), for example, are said to attract aphid-eating hoverflies.

Opposite, top left & Opposite, bottom left: Nasturtiums such as *Tropaeolum majus* 'Strawberry Ice' can be a useful sacrificial 'trap' crop attracting aphids away from legumes (here pea 'Shiraz'), tomatoes and brassicas (here kale 'Nero di Toscana'). It also encourages predatory insects like lacewings, which feast on aphids.

Opposite, top right: The flowers of onions (*Allium*), chives (*A. schoenoprasum*) and garlic (*A. sativum*) attract lots of pollinating insects. When grown under roses, they're said to help prevent blackspot.

Opposite, bottom right: Because of their pungent smell, many gardeners use French marigolds (here *Tagetes patula* 'Safari Mixture') to deter whitefly from glasshouse crops like tomatoes and chillies.

Index

Acknowledgements

Many thanks to all at Mitchell Beazley, especially Alison Starling, Leanne Bryan and Juliette Norsworthy; to Lizzie Ballantyne and Joanna Chisholm; and to the Royal Horticultural Society, particularly Rae Spencer-Jones, Simon Maughan, Leigh Hunt and Chris Young, for their tireless energy, enthusiasm and help in making this book a reality.

Special thanks to Marianne Majerus for her brilliant photography, and also to Bennet Smith. Thanks also to the designers and garden-makers featured in this book for their time and interest.

For help with the practical projects thanks to RHS Garden Wisley, particularly Matthew Pottage; Tom Wheatcroft at Capel Manor; Garden Beet (www.gardenbeet.com); Burgon & Ball (www.burgonandball.com); and Vertigro (www.vertigro.co.uk).

Lastly, thanks to Jacquie Drewe and Gordon Wise at Curtis Brown. And to my family, particularly Andria, Ellie, Frankie and Rosie for their support, encouragement and for helping me see the funny side.

GARDEN DESIGN CREDITS

Acres Wild 31; Adam Caplin 28; Adam Frost 16–17; Adam Woolcott, Jonathan Smith 172; Adrian Hallam, Chris Arrowsmith, Nigel Dunnett 208–209; Aileen Scoular 73 top, 164, 173; Alan Swann and Ahmed Farooqui 160–161; Andrew Wilson 104; Andrew Wilson and Gavin McWilliam 157 left; Andy Sturgeon 182–183, 184; Angela Kreeger 14–15; Ann Mollo 39, 84 top, 188–189; Ann Pearce 34–35, 136 bottom; Arne Maynard 179 bottom; Barbara Hunt 18–19; Barbara Schwartz 117; Bowles and Wyer 187; Bunny Guinness 166, 171; Carine Reckinger-Thill 38–39; Catherine Heatherington 64–65, 65 top, 65 bottom, 144–145; Catherine Horwood 2, 98; Catherine MacDonald 115 middle; Charlotte Rowe 34, 44–45, 45 top left, 45 top right, 45 bottom, 46–47, 51, 72 bottom, 82–83, 83 top, 83 bottom, 84 bottom, 87 top, 130, 136 top, 178, 195; Chris Ghyselen 198–199; Christopher Bradley-Hole 10, 36–37, 37 top left, 37 top right, 37 bottom, 193, 201; Christopher Masson 47 bottom; Claire Lewis 79 top; Claire Mee 52–53, 53 top, 53 bottom, 54 top, 85, 93 bottom, 176–177, 180; Cleve West 114;

Daniela Coray 141; Daniela Moderini and Laura Zampieri 22–23; David Matzdorf 148–149; Declan Buckley 74–75, 75 top left, 75 top right, 75 bottom, 77 bottom, 105; del Buono Gazerwitz Landscape Architecture 6, 43, 60–61, 61 top, 61 bottom, 71 top, 80–81, 118–119, 120–121, 134–135, 200; Diana Yakeley 96–97; Don Mapp 165 bottom; Emma Plunket 29 bottom; Emma Plunket/Scotscape 150, 150–151; Fiona Heyes 90–91; Fiona Naylor 67–68; Furzelea, Essex 202–203; Gay Wilson 153; George Carter 94 left, 94 right, 95; Gillian Blachford 24–25 bottom; Heather Culpan and Nicola Reed 167; Ian Kitson 30; Ian Kitson, Julie Toll 42 bottom, 112–113; James Lee 92–93; Jane Brockbank 55 bottom, 138–139, 146, 211 top; Jean and Simone Hoss 78 top; Jihae Hwang 13 top; Jilayne Rickards 32, 73 bottom; Jill Billington 91, 212; Jinny Blom 106 top, 118; Jo Thompson 124 top; Joe Swift 203 top; Jon Baillie 203 bottom; Julie Toll 72 top, 156; Kate Gould 12–13; Kathy Brown 186; Kim and Stephen Rogers 163 right; Laara Copley-Smith 50 left; Laurie Chetwood and Patrick Collins 58–59; Leslie Sayers 86 left; Linda Pebody 209; Luciano Giubbilei 113 top; Lucy Sommers 21, 158; Lynne Marcus 4–5,

62–63, 88 left, 88 right, 89, 124 bottom, 131, 147, 152 top, 159; Marcus Barnett 115 top; Margaret Archibald, Val Donnelly, Rae McNab, Coralin Pearson 121; Marianne Jacoby 63; Marie Clarke 93 top; Matt James 126–127; Michele Osborne 33 bottom, 68; Modular 47 top; Nigel Dunnett 13 bottom; Noel Kingsbury 210 left, 210 right; Paolo Pejrone 108–109; Paul and Patsy Harrington 78 bottom; Paul Gazerwitz 8–9, 59; Paul Southern 42 top; Peter Berg 29; Randle Siddeley 50 right; René Meyers 87 bottom; Renella Palmer 70–71; Rupert Wheeler, Paul Gazerwitz 48 left, 48 right, 49; Ruth Collier 99; Ruth Willmott and Frederic Whyte 24; Sam Martin 54 top, 161; Sara Jane Rothwell 20–21, 69, 81, 100–101, 101 right, 106 bottom, 125, 181 top; Sarah Eberle 19; Spencer Viner 24–25 top, 71 bottom; Stuart Craine 55 top, 56–57, 57 top, 57 bottom, 202, 205 top; Sue Townsend 26–27, 107, 137, 143; Susan Bennett and Earl Hyde 111 bottom right, 179 top; Theresa Mary Morton 113 bottom; Tom Stuart-Smith 40 left, 40 right, 41, 102–103, 108; Ulf Nordfjell 157 top; Val Bourne 33 second from bottom, 129 top; Vanna Colling 86 right; Vivienne Parry 11.

P. 15 REFERENCES

1. Cameron, RWF, Blanusa, T, Taylor, JE, Salisbury, A, Halstead, AJ, Henricot, B, Thompson, K, 'The domestic garden – its contribution to urban green infrastructure', *Urban Forestry and Urban Greening* 11 (2012), 129–37; Davies, ZG, Fuller, RA, Loram, A, Irvine, KN, Sims, V, Gaston, KJ, 'A national scale inventory of resource provision for biodiversity within domestic gardens', *Biological Conservation* 142 (2009), 761–71; Thompson, K, Hodgson, JG, Smith, RM, Warren, PH, Gaston, KJ, 'Urban domestic gardens (III): Composition and diversity of lawn floras', *Journal of Vegetation Science* 15 (2004), 373–8.

2. Loram, A, Tratalos, J, Warren, PH, Gaston, KJ, 'Urban domestic gardens (X): the extent & structure of the resource in five major cities', *Landscape Ecology* 22 (2007), 601–15.

3. Gill, SE, Handley, JF, Ennos, AR, Pauleit, S, 'Adapting cities for climate change:

the role of green infrastructure', *Built Environment* 33 (2007), 115–33.

4. Blanusa, T, *Gardening matters: Urban Gardens*, (RHS, 2011), 8.

5. Smith, RM, Gaston, KJ, Warren, PH, Thompson, K, 'Urban domestic gardens (VIII): environmental correlates of invertebrate abundance', *Biodiversity and Conservation* 15 (2006a), 2515–45; Smith, RM, Warren, PH, Thompson, K, Gaston, KJ, 'Urban domestic gardens (VI): environmental correlates of invertebrate species richness', *Biodiversity and Conservation* 15 (2006c), 2415–38.

6. Gregory, RD, Baillie, SR, 'Large-scale habitat use of some declining British birds', *Journal of Applied Ecology* 35 (1998), 785–99; Mason, CF, 'Thrushes now largely restricted to the built environment in eastern England', *Diversity and Distributions* 6 (2000), 189–94.

7. Owen, J, *Wildlife of a Garden: A Thirty-Year Study*, (RHS, 2010).

8. Cameron, RWF, Blanusa, T, Taylor, JE, Salisbury, A, Halstead, AJ, Henricot, B, Thompson, K, 'The domestic garden – its contribution to urban green infrastructure', *Urban Forestry and Urban Greening* 11 (2012), 129–37.

9. McCall, A, Doar, N, 'The State of Scottish Greenspace', in *Scot. Nat. Heritage Rev.* 88 (1997), Edinburgh.

10. Smith, C, *London: Garden City?* London Wildlife Trust, Greenspace Information for Greater London, Greater London Authority (2010), 12.

11. Domene, E, Sauri, D, 'Urbanisation and Water Consumption: Influencing Factors in the Metropolitan Region of Barcelona', *Urban Studies* 43 (2006), 1605–23; Syme, GJ, Shao, QX, Po, M, Campbell, E, 'Predicting and understanding home garden water use', *Landscape and Urban Planning* 68 (2004), 121–8.